Stranger Than Fiction

An Independent Investigation Of The True Culprits Behind 9-11

Stranger Than Fiction

An Independent Investigation Of The True Culprits Behind 9-11

Albert D. Pastore, Ph.D

A Dandelion Books Publication
www.dandelionbooks.net
Tempe, Arizona

A Dandelion Books Publication
Dandelion Books, LLC
Tempe, Arizona

Library of Congress Cataloging-in-Publication Data

Pastore, Albert D.
Stranger than fiction: an independent investigation of the true culprits behind 9-11

Library of Congress Catalog Card Number 2003107247
ISBN 1-893302-47-4

Cover and book design by Amnet-Systems Private, Ltd.,
www.amnet-systems.com

Disclaimer and Reader Agreement

Reader Agreement for Accessing This Book

Dandelion Books, LLC
www.dandelionbooks.net

"All truth passes through three stages. First it is ridiculed, second it is violently opposed, and third, it is accepted as self-evident."
—Arthur Schopenhauer,
German Philosopher [1788–1860]

"History is indeed little more than the register of the crimes, follies, and misfortunes of mankind."
—Edward Gibbon,
British Historian [1737–1794],
The Decline and Fall of the Roman Empire

"The most dangerous man, to any government, is the man who is able to think things out for himself . . . Almost inevitably, he comes to the conclusion that the government he lives under is dishonest, insane and intolerable."
—H.L. Mencken,
American Writer [1880–1956]

Osama Bin Laden!

You and your Al-Qaeda organization stand accused of the horrific crime which will forever be remembered in the annals of world history as "9-11."

To the charge of masterminding, organizing, and financing the mass killing of 3000 human beings, how does the defendant plead?

"I was not involved in the September 11 attacks in the United States nor did I have knowledge of the attacks. There exists a government within a government within the United States. The United States should try to trace the perpetrators of these attacks within itself; to the people who want to make the present century a century of conflict between Islam and Christianity. That secret government must be asked as to who carried out the attacks." [Source: BBC Monitoring Service/Unmat Interview, Sept. 28, 2001]

Let the trial begin!

Contents

1

Opening Statement

Socrates, the Greek philosopher, taught his students that the pursuit of truth can only begin once they start to question and analyze every belief they ever held dear.

If a certain belief passes the tests of evidence, deduction, and logic, it should be kept. If it does not, the belief should not only be discarded, but the thinker must also then question why he was led to believe the erroneous information in the first place, and for what purpose.

Not surprisingly, this type of teaching didn't sit well with the ruling elite of Greece. Many political leaders throughout history have sought to sway the masses for reasons both "good" and "bad." Socrates was tried for "subversion" and for "corrupting the youth." He was then forced to take his own life by drinking poison. It has never been easy to be an independent thinker!

Today, our ruling government/media complex does not kill people for pursuing the truth about the world (at least not yet). They simply label them as "extremists" or "paranoid," destroying careers and reputations in the process. For many, this is a fate equal to drinking hemlock.

Every news story in this book is true and easily verifiable. My investigation represents 12 months of careful study, painstaking research, detailed analysis, source verification and logical deduction. Every event and quote presented here is 100% accurate. I have included approximately 300 detailed footnotes which I encourage—urge you to explore and verify for yourself.

The Internet will enable you to obtain instant verification for every footnote by simply entering the key search words I have provided at the end of this book, into the Yahoo.com or Google.com search engines. Although possibly some of these links have already "mysteriously" disappeared, fortunately this information has been transcribed by many other websites and has therefore been preserved from censorship.

These footnote searches will take you directly to news stories reported by well-known media organizations throughout the world. They will also open doors to a world of knowledge and information that has been concealed from the general public.

In compiling this research, I purposely limited footnotes to mostly "mainstream" national and international sources (CBS, ABC, NBC, CNN, Fox News, *Washington Post, New York Times, Time, Newsweek, Jerusalem Post, Ha'Aretz* (Israel), PBS, BBC, *London Telegraph*, etc., as well as some local US newspapers and TV News stations). Let no follower of the "mainstream media" ever accuse me of using "questionable sources."

The pattern of these unusual stories is always the same. First, a curious reporter from a major media organization will report on an amazing, blockbuster story. Then, after the story has penetrated the initial media screen, forces higher up in the media organization will "spike" the story before it gains a wider audience. In some cases, this is done by an act of overt censorship. But more often, the coverup is subtly achieved by simply letting the story die on its own by not "giving it legs." Because constant repetition is the foundation of all successful advertising and marketing, a story that is reported only once or twice—no matter how sensational—will quickly fade from public memory long before it has a chance to leave a lasting impression.

In other cases, it is not the story itself that is noteworthy, but rather a particular bit of important data buried deep within. Most readers will focus on the headlines only, skimming an article and seldom reading it from start to finish. It is a sad commentary on the deteriorating state of the American intellect that we always insist upon boiling complex matters down to a headline, a slogan, a bumper sticker, a newspaper editorial, or one of those superficial 30-minute infomercials known as "The Evening News."

By carefully examining every sentence of a written news story, separating the unsubstantiated hearsay from factual details, we often find that the underemphasized portions turn out to be far more important than the overemphasized headline. Only by sifting through huge amounts of news data on a daily basis was I able to catch many of these rare "diamonds in the rough" and organize them into a coherent pattern and logical argument.

This research can literally be described as "above cover" Intelligence work. Many of the world's top Intelligence services are known to actually dedicate time and resources to scrutinizing what they refer to as "the open media" in this manner. With some common sense and a few mouse clicks, Google or Yahoo search engines on the Internet now enable anyone with an ounce of curiosity to become a Sherlock Holmes.

This book is a collection of buried but undeniable facts, events and quotes which, when assembled, state their own conclusions. In compiling this research in a logical and sequential format, great care was taken to confirm, double confirm, and triple confirm every piece of information. Any and all questionable data that could not be independently verified to this author's satisfaction was discarded. The discriminating reader will find that this investigation meets the highest standards for meticulous and truthful research.

Taken individually, each story, quote and event is highly intriguing and thought provoking. Taken collectively, the mountain of facts weaves together a clear pattern of evidence that should hammer home the truth to even the most skeptical reader.

Of course, some have fallen under the hypnotic spell of the TV talking-heads and "experts" whom they worship as authority figures. Unaccustomed to thinking for themselves, no amount of truth can sway them from their preconceived prejudices and conditioned reactions. They will even deny that which they see with their own eyes. Individuals who have been so conditioned can only parrot opinions that have been implanted in their minds by outside suggestion. In effect, millions of American minds have been reduced to the intellectual level of a CD player, spinning an implanted disc designed by outside forces of which the intended target has no awareness. They soon become victims of a psychological affliction known as "the lemming effect." Lemmings are small rodents that have been observed to follow each other as they charge to their deaths—into raging rivers or even off cliffs. Lemminghood is an innate psychological phenomenon, present in most mammals and observable in common people as well the most sophisticated and educated elites.

Lemminghood is not an intellectual phenomenon; it is psychological. As such, no socio-economic class is immune to its strangulating effect. A grant-seeking university scientist can be a lemming just as much as a fashion obsessed teen-age girl. One blindly follows the latest trendy theory while the other follows the latest clothing style. What is the difference? Neither can resist the force of nature. The power to fit in with one's social peers can be irresistible. To a human lemming, the logic behind an opinion doesn't count as much as the power and popularity behind an opinion.

Humans, like lemmings, behave collectively. Lemminghood is a necessary, sociological survival trait, an inborn instinct. Without it, humans may not have achieved even the smallest steps toward civilization. However, as with most natural phenomena, this tendency can be manipulated and used for harmful purposes. The same lemming effect that enables the masses of a justly governed society to progress toward positive, constructive ends, can just as readily self-sabotage or self-destruct.

This research work will likely be wasted on many lemmings. For lemmings, denial is a basic psychological defense mechanism used not only to shield themselves from unpleasant realities, but also to reassure themselves that they will still fit within the acceptable range of opinion held by their peer group. At all costs, their beliefs must always be on the "right" side of the issue and conform within the boundaries of their lemming peers. Lemmings simply cannot bear the burden of responsibility, or the social discomfort that comes with thinking independently. They are capable only of repeating that which they hear from the talking heads and "experts" on TV.

Lemmings will not only resist efforts to change their misguided beliefs with all of their mental energy; they will usually attack anyone who dares to question their myths. Lemmings are absolutely terrified at the thought of being labeled as an "extremist" or a "conspiracy theorist." Ironically, the very same lemmings who instinctively ridicule "conspiracy theories" are always the first ones to blindly swallow the most ridiculous conspiracy theories imaginable when the government and media present them! We can try to open the closed minds of lemmings and free them from their self-imposed blindness, but it is not easy fighting the forces of Pavlovian conditioning and human nature. The chains of ideological conformity have too strong a grip, and breaking them is a difficult task.

Lemmings have been conditioned to obediently grovel before the "authority" of their media and government masters. With the limited resources at our disposal, it is next to impossible to compete with these masters. For this reason, the lie of the emperor is always believed before the truth of the peasant. Nevertheless, some of us must make the meager attempt, and thus lay the foundation upon which the truth might one day rise again.

This is not to suggest that those who have been misinformed are lemmings. Anyone can be fooled if the information they are receiving is inaccurate or incomplete. There is no shame in being misinformed. On the other hand, to stubbornly persist in erroneous thinking even after the irrefutable evidence and logic have been presented, is the essence of lemminghood.

A few persons do possess the intelligence, strength and nobility of character to break free from lemminghood and to admit they were once badly fooled. They also have the courage to then face the sad fact that they were inmates trapped in a global insane asylum. Those individuals who can muster up these moral and mental virtues will then be ready to accept the truth when it is presented in clear and logical sequence.

To those open-minded, independent thinkers I wish to state clearly and unequivocally that I intend to set forth in this book an overwhelming body of evidence which should forever destroy the ridiculous notion that a Saudi caveman and his band of half-trained, nerdy Arab flight school students, orchestrated the most sophisticated terror operation in world history. The very idea is utterly laughable. And yet, due to the blithering barrage of bovine excrement dished out by the government/media complex, millions now accept this fantastic fairy tale, this silly superstition, this dangerous delusion, with a zealous conviction bordering on mass insanity.

As a probably useless public service to my helplessly doomed countrymen, and as a gift to a posterity which will hopefully be more enlightened than my bewildered, blood-thirsty, flag-waving contemporaries, I have presented this research with the hope of liberating as many people as I can from the oppressive yoke of media brainwashing and state-sponsored lies.

Do you have what it takes to break free from the lemming mob? If so, read on!

2

The Dancing Israelis

Like most Americans, I was gripped by profound shock, revulsion, rage—and sadness—as I watched the horror of September 11, 2001 unfolding live on my television screen. Witnessing the mass murder of thousands of innocent people was the most upsetting experience of my life.

How could any person of sound moral character not be enraged? To read about some faraway, long-ago genocide in a newspaper or book is distressing enough. But to actually see before one's eyes, the mass murder of what was at first believed to have been tens of thousands of innocent people—fortunately the actual numbers turned out to be much lower—is truly traumatic.

I barely slept for two nights afterwards and suffered nightmares. I tried to imagine what it would have been like to have to telephone my family for the last time before jumping out of a quarter mile high burning building; my remains to be smashed upon the New York pavement like a scrambled egg.

What horror. Polling data would later reveal that 65% of Americans actually shed tears on 9-11.[1]

Not all of the eye-witnesses to the 9-11 slaughter were so saddened and sobered. On September 11, five Israeli army veterans were arrested by the FBI after several witnesses saw them "dancing," "high-five-ing" and "celebrating" as they took pictures of the World Trade Center disaster from across the river in New Jersey. Steven Gordon was the lawyer who volunteered to represent the five Israelis. He was asked by a Hebrew newspaper why the five men were being detained by the FBI. Here's what Gordon told *Yediot America*:

> "On the day of the disaster, three of the five boys went up on the roof of the building where the company office is located," said Gordon. "I'm not sure if they saw the twin towers collapse, but, in any event, they photographed the ruins right afterwards. One of the neighbors who saw them called the police and claimed they were posing, dancing and laughing, against the background of the burning towers ...
>
> "Anyhow, the three left the roof, took an Urban truck, and drove to a parking lot, located about a five-minute drive from the offices. They parked, stood on the roof of the truck to get a better view of the destroyed towers and took photographs. A woman who was in the building above the lot testified that she saw them smiling and exchanging high-fives. She and another neighbor called the police and reported on Middle-Eastern looking people dancing on the truck. They copied and reported the license plates."[2]

The *Ha'aretz* news service of Israel reported:

> The Foreign Ministry said it had been informed by the consulate in New York that the FBI had arrested the five for "puzzling behavior." They are said to have had been caught videotaping the disaster and shouting in what was interpreted as cries of joy and mockery.[3]

Ha'aretz described how FBI field agents then subjected the five Israelis to many days of brutal interrogation, torture, and solitary confinement. When their photos were developed, it was revealed that the dancing Israelis were smiling in the foreground of the New York massacre.[4] According to ABC's 20/20 attempted whitewash of the incident, in addition to their outrageous and highly suspicious behavior, the five also had in their possession the following items: box-cutters, European passports, and $4700 cash hidden in a sock.[5]

Why were these Israelis so happy about the horrible massacre that was unfolding right before their very eyes? What evil spirit could possess people who are supposed to be America's "allies" and who receive billions of dollars in financial and military aid from US taxpayers each year, to publicly rejoice as innocent people (including many American Jews) were burning to death and jumping out of 110-story buildings? Could it be that these happy Israeli army vets were in some way linked to this monstrous attack? That's what officials close to the investigation initially told the *Bergen Record* newspaper of New Jersey.

The *Record* reported on September 12, 2001 that the Israelis were initially spotted at New Jersey's Liberty State Park at the time of the initial crash. For those unfamiliar with the NY-NJ area, it should be noted that Liberty Park, located directly across the river, offers the clearest and most unobstructed view possible of the World Trade Center. It would be the ideal place to position yourself if you had advance knowledge of an attack and wanted to witness it. In an article titled "Five Men Detained as Suspected Conspirators," the *Bergen Record* reported:

> Sources said the FBI alert, known as a BOLO or "Be On Lookout," was sent out at 3:31 PM. It read:

> "Vehicle possibly related to New York terrorist attack. White, 2000 Chevrolet van with New Jersey registration with 'Urban Moving Systems' sign on back seen at Liberty State Park, Jersey City, NJ, at the time of first impact of jetliner into World Trade Center.

> Three individuals with van were seen celebrating after initial impact and subsequent explosion. FBI Newark Field Office requests that, if the van is located, hold for prints and detain individuals." [6]

As incredible, as ridiculous, and as "paranoid" as the idea of Israeli involvement in 9-11 may seem, the fact is that certain elements within the Israeli government, and International Zionist movement in general, have a long history of attacking the US and framing Arabs in order to gain support from the US. Before we begin to piece together what really transpired on 9-11, it is absolutely critical that we first review some historical precedents regarding Israel's and International Zionism's treacherous history of manipulating America—and other nations—for their own selfish purposes. Without a basic understanding of this history, it would be impossible to understand the truth as it is today. So put aside your preconceived notions, your psychological defense mechanisms and your prejudices, and step into my time machine for an unforgettable journey down the memory hole of history.

3

Zionism and World War I

In the latter part of the 1800s, there arose in Europe a political movement known as "Zionism." Zionism in particular referred to the effort among certain Jews to establish a Jewish nation in the land of Palestine. Today, the term Zionism is more commonly applied to those Jews who want to expand the borders of what was already established, at the expense of the Palestinians who once owned the land.

In a more general sense, the term "Zionist" is also used to describe a segment of the Jewish community who believe in Jewish Supremacy, thus putting their own interests ahead of those of any nation in which they reside. It is a mistake to assume that all Jews are supporters of the "Zionist Mafia" or Jewish Supremacy. In fact, some of the strongest condemnations of Zionism, Israeli brutality, and Jewish Supremacy come from Jews themselves.

On the Internet and often in books that do make it through the media and book industry's subtle form of censorship known among publishers as "sandbagging," one can read articles and books by the large number of anti-Zionist authors, historians, and journalists, including John Sack,[1] Alfred Lilienthal,[2] Noam Chomsky,[3] Israel Shahak,[4] Benjamin Freedman,[5] Jack Bernstein,[6] Henry Makow,[7] and Victor Ostrovsky.[8]

Jews against Zionism have even formed a group called "Neturei Karta."[9] For their brave efforts, these men have had to tolerate vicious abuse from Zionist smear groups such as the Anti-Defamation League (ADL)—an organization which actually specializes in slander, defamation, and spying for Israel! Author Jack Bernstein described the abusive ADL smear process and challenged his fellow Jews as follows:

> I am well aware of the tactics YOU, my Zionist brethren, use to quiet anyone who attempts to expose any of your subversive acts. If the person is a gentile, you cry, "You're anti-Semitic," which is nothing more than a smokescreen to hide your actions. But if a Jew is the person doing the exposing, you resort to other tactics:
>
> • First, you ignore the charges, hoping the information will not be given widespread distribution.
> • If the information starts reaching too many people, you ridicule the information and the person giving the information.
> • If that doesn't work, your next step is character assassination. If the author or speaker hasn't been involved in sufficient scandal, you are adept at fabricating a scandal against the person or persons.
> • If none of these is effective, you are known to resort to physical attacks.

> But NEVER do you try to prove the information wrong. So, before you commence efforts to silence me, I offer this challenge: You Zionists assemble a number of Zionist Jews and witnesses to support your position; and I will assemble a like number of anti-Zionist, pro-American Jews and witnesses.

> Then, the Zionists and anti-Zionists will state their positions and debate the material in this book as well as related material—and the debate WILL BE HELD ON PUBLIC TELEVISION. Let's explore the information both sides can

present and let the American people decide for themselves if the information is true or false. ISN'T THAT A FAIR CHALLENGE?

Certainly, you will willingly accept the challenge if what I have written is false. But if you resort to crying "Lies, all lies" and refuse to debate, you will, in effect, be telling the American people that what I have written here are the true facts.[10]

Needless to say, Bernstein's challenge was never accepted. So let us put to rest now and forever the slanderous lie, and strategic Zionist propaganda ploy that labels anyone who dares to call attention to the dangers of the Zionist Mafia an "anti-Semite," "hatemonger," or a "skin-head."

This dirty trick of screaming "anti-Semitism" at the first sign of criticism serves three important strategic purposes for the Zionists:

1. It intimidates and paralyzes their opposition into silence and inaction.
2. It instills a negative Pavlovian reaction in the public mind— a conditioned "knee-jerk" response which prevents people who oppose bigotry from ever pausing to take a critical look at the true facts.
3. It keeps their fellow Jews in a constant state of fear and anxiety. This keeps them cohesive and vulnerable to Zionist control.

In essence, the Zionist Mafia uses the unwitting masses of the Jewish people as unsuspecting "human shields" to conceal their criminal and treasonous activities. Although many Jews have become wise to this dirty Zionist trick, most, unfortunately, have been duped since early childhood.

Zionists in the late 1800s faced one small problem with their bold takeover scheme of Arab Palestine. Palestine was under the sovereignty of the Ottoman Turkish Empire and the Arabs of Palestine certainly weren't about to just give away prime real estate in Palestine to the Zionists of Europe. Clearly, the early Zionists must have believed that some powerful nation could be persuaded to steal Palestine from the Arabs and their Ottoman sovereigns.

At the time, very few Jews were even living in Palestine, and the Jews had not controlled Palestine since the days of the Roman Empire. This destroys the commonly believed myth that the Arabs and Jews "have been fighting over that land for centuries." The handful of Arab Jews who lived in Palestine got along well with their Muslim hosts and never expressed any desire whatsoever to overthrow the Ottoman rulers and set up a nation called Israel. The movement to strip Palestine away from the Ottoman Empire came strictly from European Zionists who had become influential within several European nations.

Unless some European power could grab Palestine by force, the dream of a Jewish state would remain just that—a dream.

As fate (or design) would have it, a great opportunity would soon present itself to the Zionist Mafia. In 1914 "The Great War" pitted Germany, Austria-Hungary, and the Ottoman Turkish Empire against England, France, and Russia. The Zionists played an important role in dragging the US into that bloody European war—a war in which the US had no vital interests at stake whatsoever.

By 1916, the Germans, Austrians, and Ottoman Turks had seemingly won the war. Russia was in turmoil and about to be swallowed up by a communist revolution. France had suffered horrible losses and Britain was under a German U-boat blockade. Germany made an offer to Britain to end the war under conditions favorable to Britain.

But the British, and the international Zionists, had one more card to play. The British government and Zionist leaders, including Chaim Weizmann, the man who would one day become the first President of the State of Israel, struck a dirty deal. The Zionists would use their influence to drag the mighty US into the war on Britain's side, to crush Germany and its Ottoman allies.

In exchange for helping to bring the US into the war, the British would reward the Zionists by taking over Palestine from the conquered Ottomans after the war was over. The British had originally designated an African territory for the Jewish homeland. But the Zionists were fixated on claiming Palestine as their land. Once under British control, the Jews of Europe would be allowed to immigrate to Palestine in great numbers.

Zionists powerbrokers such as Bernard Baruch, Louis Brandeis, Paul Warburg (father of the US Federal Reserve), Jacob Schiff, and others immediately went to work to put the screws to President Woodrow Wilson. Overnight the Zionist-influenced press transformed the German Kaiser and his people into bloodthirsty "Huns" determined to destroy western civilization.

In 1916, the US, with the help of the previous year's *Lusitania* "incident," entered the war on Britain's side under the ridiculous pretext of "making the world safe for democracy."

"Beat Back the Hun!" declared Fred Strothman's famous propaganda poster—a slogan which became a rallying cry of "patriotic" Americans. Woodrow Wilson was caught up in a sinister force beyond his control—a force which he himself described years earlier in his 1913 book, *The New Freedom*:

> Since I entered politics, I have chiefly had men's views confided to me privately. Some of the biggest men in the U. S., in the field of commerce and manufacturing, are afraid of something. They know that there is a power somewhere so organized, so subtle, so watchful, so interlocked, so complete, so pervasive, that they had better not speak above their breath when they speak in condemnation of it.[11]

Meanwhile, in Germany—where this Zionist force also wielded tremendous influence in the press and industry—enthusiasm for the war was suddenly watered down by Zionist-run newspapers. Ironically, these were the same Zionist newspapers that had previously been in favor of a German war against the hated Czar of Russia, the arch enemy of the Zionists/Bolsheviks at that time. But when it became apparent that the theft of Palestine was within reach, the Zionists of Germany did a 360-degree turnaround.

Zionist and Marxist union leaders organized wartime labor strikes in German weapons factories. With the German branch of the International Zionist Mafia undermining German war efforts and German morale from within, and the English and American branches of the Zionist mafia pushing America to join the war, it wasn't long before the German, Austrian, and Ottoman Empires were defeated and their maps rewritten by the victorious powers at the infamous Treaty of Versailles in 1918. In addition to the numerous Zionist bankers who were influencing Versailles, the Zionists also had their own delegation which was headed by Chaim Weizmann. Great Britain issued the Balfour Declaration in November 1917, one year before Germany surrendered. It had actually been prepared 20 months earlier in March 1916 with Weizmann's influence.[12]

The Declaration allowed mass Jewish immigration to conquered Palestine while promising to preserve Arab rights. The Arabs living in Palestine weren't buying these promises. They protested, but there was nothing they could do to stop the wave of Jewish immigration. This was the first step in creating what 30 years later was to become the State of Israel.

Years after the war, an American Zionist millionaire named Benjamin Freedman broke ranks with his fellow Zionists and turned against them. Freedman was the principal owner of the Woodbury Soap Company and was one of the many Zionists present at the Treaty of Versailles. Freedman was well connected and had enjoyed access to several US presidents. He became disgusted with the criminal behavior of the Zionist mafia and dedicated much of his life and fortune to exposing the truth about both World Wars and the Zionist grip on America. According to Freedman, Wilson had been blackmailed by Zionists with the threat of a public disclosure of an extramarital affair Wilson had had when he was president of Princeton University.[13]

Freedman's voluminous (and buried) writings, speeches, and books on this subject are essential reading (if you can find them!). One leader of the Anti-Defamation League, Arnold Forster, once smeared Freedman as a "self-hating Jew."[14]

Following is a brief excerpt from a 1961 speech that Freedman gave before an audience at the Willard Hotel in Washington DC in which he described the forces at work behind America's entry into World War I:

> The Zionists in Germany, who represented the Zionists from Eastern Europe, went to the British War Cabinet and—I am going to be brief because it's a long story, but

I have all the documents to prove any statement that I make—they said: "Look here. You can yet win this war.

"You don't have to give up. You don't have to accept the negotiated peace offered to you now by Germany. You can win this war if the United States will come in as your ally."

The United States was not in the war at that time. We were fresh; we were young; we were rich; we were powerful. They told England: "We will guarantee to bring the United States into the war as your ally, to fight with you on your side, if you will promise us Palestine after you win the war."

In other words, they made this deal: "We will get the United States into this war as your ally. The price you must pay is Palestine after you have won the war and defeated Germany, Austria-Hungary, and Turkey."

It is absolutely absurd that Great Britain, that never had any connection to, interest or right in what is known as Palestine, should offer it as coin of the realm to pay the Zionists for bringing the United States into the war. However, they did make that promise, in October of 1916. And shortly after that, the United States, which was almost totally pro-German, entered the war as Britain's ally.[15]

We may debate as to exactly what extent this Zionist-British dirty deal was responsible for dragging the sons of America off to die in a European bloodbath. Some, including Freedman, believe it was the only reason the US entered the war. Others, including this writer, believe it was the primary contributing factor. But let us at this point agree on this one irrefutable point: the Zionists had no aversion to seeing Americans die for their own selfish interests. Even the *Encyclopedia Britannica* and *Microsoft Encarta Encyclopedia* (look under "Balfour Declaration") confirm this little known fact of World War I. Here's the excerpt from *Microsoft Encarta*:

THE BALFOUR DECLARATION. The Balfour Declaration was a letter prepared in March 1916 and issued in

November 1917, during World War I, by the British statesman Arthur James Balfour, then foreign secretary ... Specifically, the letter expressed the British government's approval of Zionism with "the establishment in Palestine of a national home for the Jewish people." The letter committed the British government to making the "best endeavors to facilitate the achievement of this object, it being clearly understood that nothing shall be done to prejudice the rights of existing non-Jewish communities in Palestine."

The immediate purpose was to win for the Allied cause in World War I the support of Jews in the warring nations and in the United States. As a result of the Balfour Declaration, Israel was established as an independent state in 1948 in the mandated area.[16]

It is also worth mentioning at this point that when the British dismantled the Ottoman Empire after World War I, they created many smaller nations. They formed the oil rich puppet kingdom of Kuwait by slicing off the southern coastal tip of what we now know as the nation of Iraq. As a result of this arbitrary redrawing of the Ottoman map, a bitter conflict was created between Iraq and Kuwait. Iraq has always considered Kuwait its true southern province. This, along with Kuwait's "slant drilling" theft of Iraqi oil, ultimately led to Iraq's invasion of Kuwait in 1991 and the subsequent Gulf War.

4

Zionism and World War II

Let us fast forward our time machine to the early 1930s. Again, there is no need for a detailed analysis and debate of the causes and major events of World War II. The sole purpose here is to illustrate yet another case of selfish Zionist agitation for American entry into a war.

The German people were bitterly resentful of not only the Zionist role in bringing about their defeat in World War I, but also of the brutal monetary reparations imposed upon them by certain Zionist bankers who helped craft the Treaty of Versailles after the war. Stripped of formerly German territory, and with the German economy in ruins, the people of Germany elected Adolf Hitler as their Chancellor in 1932. Hitler and the Nazi party soon seized control of the German media, banks, and universities from the influential Zionists who had reigned supreme in those institutions.

Almost immediately, Zionists throughout the world began to agitate for action against Germany. Boycotts of German imports were imposed and calls for the UK and USA to take immediate action against Germany began to emanate from Zionist circles. On March 24, 1933 (6 years before the war began!) the *Daily Express* of England carried the bold headline: "Judea Declares War on Germany; Jews of All the World Unite in Action."[1] The front page story revealed that the Zionists had announced a concerted worldwide effort to isolate

Germany and turn other nations against her. The following year, Zionist political leader Vladimir Jabotinksy wrote:

> The fight against Germany has now been waged for months by every Jewish community, on every continent ... We shall start a spiritual and material war of the world against Germany. Our Jewish interests call for the complete destruction of Germany.[2]

A few years later, Lord Beaverbrook, a British newspaper magnate issued this warning about the Zionist influence over the British press:

> There are 20,000 German Jews who have come here to England. They all work against an agreement with Germany. The Jews have got a big position in the press here. Their political influence is driving us into the direction of war.[3]

In September of 1939, Germany and Poland went to war over disputed territory that was taken away from Germany by the Versailles Treaty of 1918. Under the phony pretext of protecting Poland, Great Britain and France immediately declared war on Germany (conveniently ignoring the fact that Stalin's Soviet Union had also invaded Poland). Germany pleaded with Britain and France (the Allies) to withdraw their war declarations, but to no avail. The Allies continued their massive military buildup along Germany's frontiers. Germany's neighbors (Belgium, Holland and also Norway) came under intense Allied political pressure to allow Allied armies to establish bases in their territories. In the spring of 1940, the war in Western Europe began when Germany launched pre-emptive invasions of Norway, Holland, and Belgium, pinning the British and French forces on the beaches of Belgium before they were boat-lifted across the English Channel. Beaverbrook's prediction was realized.

In the United States, the Zionist Mafia again went to work on a US president. The names of the players had changed but the game was still the same. Baruch was still pulling presidential strings along with other Zionist "advisors," including Henry Morgenthau, Eugene Myer, and Harold Ickes. Myer, a business associate of

Baruch, bought the *Washington Post* during this time. (Myer's grandson Donald Graham runs the *Post* today.) For his part, Ickes, FDR's Secretary of the Interior, banned the sale of helium to Germany in 1934. This forced the Germans to use flammable hydrogen to operate their famous airships. The Hindenburg Airship disaster of 1937 was due in large part to Harold Ickes' vindictive helium sanctions against Germany.

It was Franklin Delano Roosevelt's turn to deliver the US into another European war. Patriotic Americans including famed aviator Charles Lindbergh saw this and tried to warn the American people that Zionist media influence was intending to drive us into another World War. Said Lindbergh:

> I am not attacking the Jewish people. But I am saying that the leaders of both the British and the Jewish races, for reasons which are as understandable from their viewpoint as they are inadvisable from ours, for reasons which are not American, wish to involve us in the war.[4]

Because of strong public anti-war sentiment, as well as the growing realization that World War I was a total waste, FDR and his Zionist handlers were having a difficult time dragging the US into another bloody European war. It would take a serious "incident" to get the USA into World War II.

Germany had wisely refused to respond to FDR's provocations (impounding of German vessels, assisting the British in attacking German ships, etc.) so FDR began baiting Japan instead. Japan and Germany were bound to a mutual defense agreement, which meant that war with Japan would automatically mean war with Germany. This gave FDR a "back-door" to get into the war. He shut down the "neutral" Panama Canal to Japanese shipping, ordered US battleships to cruise through Japanese waters, and embargoed Japan's wartime oil supply, hoping these aggressive moves would force Japan's hand.

It worked. Overwhelming evidence from government documents clearly shows that FDR had advance knowledge of the Japanese attack on Pearl Harbor and allowed it to happen so that he could drag the US into the war.[5]

After December 7, 1941, a wave of patriotic indignation swept across America and drove us into the war. As was the case in World War I, US entry led to another crushing defeat of Germany. Hours before committing suicide on April 30, 1945, Adolf Hitler dictated his last will and political testament. In it he placed responsibility for World War II on the Zionist Mafia—or, as he called it—"International Jewry and its henchmen." It is certainly no surprise that Hitler would make such a claim. However, his final accusation of the Zionists does parallel the statements made by Jabotinsky, Lindbergh, Beaverbrook, Prime Minister Neville Chamberlain, Ambassador Joe Kennedy, and many others. In the final public communication of his life, Hitler wrote:

> It is untrue that I or anyone else in Germany wanted war in 1939. It was wanted and provoked solely by international statesmen either of Jewish Origin or working for Jewish interests. Nor had I ever wished that after the appalling first World War, there would ever be a second against either England or America.[6]

Regardless of your view of World War II and whether or not the US should have participated, the essential irrefutable point is: years before World War II had even started, the Zionists had yet again demonstrated that they had no aversion to sending Americans to die for their own interests.

5

Great Britain's Turn To Be Betrayed

A few years after the end of World War II, the Zionist plan to establish the nation of Israel in Palestine was finally realized. But not before the British protectors of Palestine were chased out by Zionist acts of terror. It was British troops who unwittingly sacrificed their lives in order to steal Palestine away from Arab control, allowing the Jews of Europe to immigrate there [see World War I & Balfour Declaration, Chapter 3]. But with Great Britain left weakened and in debt from World War II, the ungrateful Zionists saw their opportunity to now chase the British out of Palestine by committing acts of terrorism against them. The most notorious of the Zionist terror groups was the Irgun, whose leader, Menachem Begin would one day become the Prime Minister of Israel and winner of the Nobel Peace Prize!

On the morning of July 22, 1946, a group of 15–20 Irgun terrorists dressed as Arabs entered the King David Hotel in Jerusalem. They unloaded 225 kilograms of explosives hidden in milk churns.[1] The King David Hotel housed the Secretariat of the Government of Palestine and Headquarters of the British Forces in Palestine. When a British officer became suspicious, a shootout took place and the Irgun lit the fuses and fled. The explosion destroyed part of the hotel and killed 91 people. Most of the victims were British but 15 innocent Jews also died, proving that radical Zionists are capable of even killing fellow Jews in order to advance their cause.

The Irgun terror gang also targeted Arab civilians in order to frighten them into evacuating their villages. The most well known of these numerous massacres happened at the village of Deir Yassin on the morning of April 9, 1948. More than 254 defenseless Christian Arabs, including many old men, women and children, were dragged out of their homes, lined up against a wall and shot. Some of the bodies were mutilated by knife-work performed by Menachem Begin's butchers.[2] After the murderous orgy was completed, Irgun, (and also Stern Gang) commandos threw the dead bodies down a well. The Israeli butchers then took over all the villages from which the terrorized Arab population fled.

Begin was not merely suspected of being behind these murderous deeds. He *admitted* that the Irgun's terror campaigns were necessary for the establishment of a Jewish state!

The sheer brutality of Begin's butchery was such that even some prominent American Jews felt compelled to speak out against Begin's subsequent visit to the United States in December of 1948. On December 8, 1948, a harshly worded open letter of protest appeared in the *New York Times*. Among the more noteworthy of the numerous signatories were Jewish scientist, Albert Einstein and Jewish writer, Hannah Arendt. Although both Einstein and Arendt were supporters of Israel, they still could not stomach the murderous policies of Mr. Begin. They wrote in the *Times*:

> Among the most disturbing political phenomena of our time is the emergence in the newly created State of Israel of "The Freedom Party"... It was formed out of the membership and following of the former Irgun, a terrorist chauvinist organization in Palestine.

> The current visit of Menachem Begin to the United States is obviously calculated to give the impression of American support for his party in the coming elections. It is inconceivable that those who oppose fascism throughout the world, if currently informed as to Mr. Begin's political record and perspectives, could add their names and support to the

movement he represents. A shocking example was their behavior in the Arab village of Deir Yassin. This incident exemplified the character and actions of the Freedom Party.

Within the Jewish community they have preached an admixture of ultra-nationalism, religious mysticism, and racial superiority ... their record of past performance in Palestine bear the imprint of no ordinary political party. This is the unmistakable stamp of a Fascist party for whom terrorism, against Jews, Arabs and British alike, and misrepresentation are means, and a "Leader State" is the goal ... It is all the more tragic that the top leadership of American Zionism has refused to campaign against Begin's efforts.[3]

Begin's visit to the US caused a firestorm of protest, but the Zionists around President Harry Truman allowed him to visit and meet with him anyway. One well-known Congressman actually withdrew his name from the welcoming committee for Begin after he learned the sickening truth about Begin's terrorist past. The Congressman sent this message to Begin's US welcoming committee:

Belatedly and for the record I wish to withdraw my name from the reception committee for Menachem Begin, the former Irgun Commander. When accepting your invitation, I was ignorant of the true nature of his activities, and I wish to be disassociated from them completely.[4]

That Congressman's name was John F. Kennedy.

By 1948, the British had had enough of Palestine. Under intense Zionist lobbying, the UN, UK and US had recognized the nation of Israel in 1948. One of the first acts of the new Israeli government was to pass "the law of return," which gives any Jew in the world the right to move to Israel and become a citizen.

Understandably, the Arab nations weren't too pleased about this. Several wars would follow. But the Israelis and their free arsenal of America's finest weapons kept the Arabs from reclaiming their stolen land. The Arabs have never been a match for the US-supplied Israeli war machine.

The irony of "the law of return" is that many of today's Jews have no direct ancestral link to the Jews of the Old Testament. Many, perhaps even most, Jewish people are descended from the Khazars, a people whose rulers converted to Judaism sometime during the 800 AD.[5] The Khazars never even set foot in Palestine!

The brutal and criminal circumstances surrounding the creation of Israel happened more than half a century ago. Even most Arabs have come to understand that Israel isn't going to go away. But by reviewing the true history of Zionist terrorism, we are now better equipped to understand the deceptive, dangerous, fanatical and brutal nature of international Zionism as it exists today. Current Israeli Prime Minister Ariel Sharon is a protégé of Menachem Begin.

6

America Becomes the Zionists' Main Whore

We saw how the Zionists used and discarded Germany, then used and discarded Great Britain. After World War II, it was clear that the chief remaining global power was the United States.

The US had never had any problem with the Arab people, and had no reason to quarrel with the Arabs. For the Zionists to maintain and expand the support they were receiving from America, it would be of great benefit if the Arabs and the mighty US could somehow become enemies. Could the Zionists possibly stoop so low? Why not? Look at what they had already pulled off! Remember that the official motto of the Mossad (Israel's intelligence organization) is "By way of deception thou shalt do war."[1]

In 1955, one of these "false flag" operations was publicly exposed for the world to see. Israeli agents impersonating Arab terrorists were caught staging a series of bombings against American installations in Egypt.[2] When this conspiracy was exposed, the Israeli government claimed it was an "anti-Semitic" hoax. But when the Egyptians produced the captured Jewish terrorists, Israel was forced to admit the existence of this "false flag" operation.

The scandal caused such a controversy that ultimately it brought down the Israeli government. The long since forgotten scandal came to be known as "the Lavon Affair," after Pinchas Lavon, the Israeli defense Minister who was blamed for failed conspiracy.

Then again, on June 8, 1967, during a war with the Arabs, Israeli gunboats and fighter jets deliberately attacked the *USS Liberty*, an unarmed US communications ship.[3] Thirty-five American sailors were murdered and 170 others injured in a prolonged Israeli onslaught—carried out in broad daylight and with the US flag flying prominently. The intent was to kill all the Americans and then leave the Egyptians to take the blame. The Israelis even machine gunned the US lifeboats. The Israelis finally had to break off the attack when they thought US fighters jets were on the way to help. Israel denied that the attack was deliberate and claimed that they mistook the American ship for an Egyptian one.

But the chilling stories of the lucky American survivors clearly contradict that lie. Admiral Thomas Moorer, Chairman of the Joint Chiefs of Staff under President Reagan, insists that the attack was deliberate. Dean Rusk, the US Secretary of State under President Johnson, also stated that the attack was no accident and was approved by highest levels of the Israel government. At the time, terrorist Menachem Begin was serving as a high ranking minister.

Evidence that the murderous attack on the *USS Liberty* was deliberate is overwhelming. The survivors of the brutal attack operate a website at www.ussliberty.org. It is an excellent resource which clearly dispels the Israeli lie that the attack on the *USS Liberty* was an "accident."

Despite the statements of prominent figures like Rusk and Moorer, and despite the unanimous testimony of the lucky survivors, the US Congress has never interviewed the survivors, nor have they ever investigated the *USS Liberty* massacre!

In the 1980s, the Israelis once again succeeded in framing enemy Arabs in order to enrage America. Former Mossad case officer, Victor Ostrovsky became so disgusted with the criminal behavior of his own government, he defected from the Mossad. Ostrovsky tried to warn America of just how evil and murderous the Mossad actually was. Ostrovsky revealed exactly how the Israelis framed

Libya for the bombing of a German night club in which American servicemen were killed.[4] It was this frame-up job that caused President Reagan to bomb Libya in 1986, killing the four-year-old daughter of Libyan leader, Muamar Qadhafi.

France refused to allow US bombers to fly over their air space and bomb Libya. A wave of anti-French sentiment swept across America. I can still recall demonstrations of angry American "patriots" dumping bottles of French wine, and radio hosts urging listeners to boycott French goods. Ignoramuses throughout America (including this writer, I'm ashamed to say) shrieked: "We bailed those Frenchies out of two World Wars and this is how they thank us!"

But the reason France refused to cooperate with the deadly US bombing raid was because French intelligence knew that Libya had been framed by the Israelis. Ostrovsky, whose 1990 tell-all book, *By Way of Deception*, infuriated the Mossad, made him the target of numerous death threats.[5] Among some of Ostrovsky's other amazing revelations are:

- The Mossad recruits Arab agents to carry out missions.
- Israeli agents are skilled at impersonating Arabs.
- Mossad had an elaborate plan to vilify Iraq and involve the US in a war against it.
- The Mossad knew in advance of the 1983 Arab surprise attack on US Marines based in Lebanon. Instead of warning their American "allies," the Mossad deliberately allowed more than 200 US Marines to be killed in the surprise bombing attack.
- Wealthy Zionists in America are often called upon to help carry out Mossad missions.

In 2001, the *Washington Times* ran a story about a 68-page research paper issued by the Army School of Advanced Military Studies (SAMS). The research was compiled by 60 US Army officers as an attempt to predict the possible outcomes of deploying a US force to maintain peace between the Israel and Palestinians. Here's what SAMS had to say about the Israeli military machine:

A 500 pound gorilla in Israel. Well armed and trained. Operates in both Gaza and the West Bank. Known to disregard international law to accomplish mission.[6]

Of Israel's Mossad, the officers issued this warning:

> Wildcard. Ruthless and cunning. Has capability to target US forces and make it look like a Palestinian Arab act.[7]

Why does the US, which is trillions of dollars in debt, give away billions of taxpayer dollars to a foreign government whose military violates international laws and whose intelligence agency is capable of murdering US troops in order to frame Arabs? Have we lost our minds?

It is hoped that the enquiring reader has already begun to ask, "Why have I never heard of these amazing events? I read newspapers. I watch the evening news, CNN, and all the Sunday morning talk shows. I read the *New York Times* and the *Wall Street Journal*. I never miss an episode of *60 Minutes*. I watch the History Channel.

"I consider myself a well-informed, educated citizen. Why was I never told about the Balfour Declaration, or the King David Hotel, or Deir Yassin? Why was I never told that Kennedy and Einstein publicly condemned Menachem Begin as a terrorist? Why was I never told of the Lavon Affair, or of the attack on the *USS Liberty*, or that Libya was framed by the Mossad? Why haven't I seen this Victor Ostrovsky fellow on TV?"

This puzzling question will be addressed in the next chapter. The worst is yet to come.

7

Zionist Power Structure in America

Now that we have established the ruthless and criminal nature of radical Zionism, one more factor needs to be understood before we return to the five dancing Israelis of 9-11 and other related stories.

Even the Zionists themselves have never denied that they have long exerted great influence in America. But what we must understand is that the Zionists do not merely influence United States policy ... they dominate it! It is this domination that has enabled them to pull off some of the monstrous crimes already described in previous chapters, and then conceal those crimes from the general public.

Many prominent Americans have observed that Zionists dominate the American media, government, academia, and Hollywood. It is easily verifiable by public information.

Henry Ford said:

> If after having elected their man or group, obedience is not rendered to the Jewish control, then you speedily hear of "scandals" and "investigations" and "impeachments" for the removal of the disobedient. Usually a man with a "past" proves the most obedient instrument, but even a good man can often be tangled up in campaign practices that compromise him. It has been commonly known that Jewish manipulation of American election campaigns has been so

skillfully handled, that no matter which candidate was elected, there was ready made a sufficient amount of evidence to discredit him in case his Jewish masters needed to discredit him.[1]

Charles Lindbergh said:

The greatest danger to this country lies in the Jewish ownership and influence in our motion pictures, our press, our radio, and our government.[2]

Admiral Thomas Moorer, Chairman of the US Joint Chiefs of Staff under Ronald Reagan said:

I've never seen a President—I don't care who he is—stand up to them [the Israelis]. It just boggles the mind. They always get what they want. The Israelis know what is going on all the time. If the American people understood what a grip those people have got on our government, they would rise up in arms. Our citizens certainly don't have any idea what goes on.[3]

While a guest on ABC's *Face the Nation*, William Fulbright—US Senator and Chairman of the US Foreign Relations committee—once said before a national audience:

Israel controls the United States Senate. We should be more concerned about the United States' interests.[4]

That remark cost Fulbright his Senate seat in the following election, a defeat for which the Israel lobby (which funded his opponent) openly took credit.

Nationally syndicated columnist and former presidential candidate, Patrick Buchanan wrote: "The United States Congress is Israeli occupied territory."[5]

And US religious leader Billy Graham and President Richard Nixon once had the following exchange, which was caught on tape:

GRAHAM: The Jewish stranglehold on the media has got to be broken or this country's going down the drain.

NIXON: You believe that?

GRAHAM: Yes, sir.

NIXON: Oh boy. So do I. I can't ever say that, but I do believe it.[6]

More recently, US Brigadier General James J. David (Ret.), in an article entitled "A Passionate Attachment to Israel," wrote:

> Is there any criminal act that Israel can do without being protected from criticism from the United States? If there is I haven't seen it. And I haven't seen it from the Bush Administration or from the Clinton Administration or from any administration before them. But when you consider the influence of Israel's lobby and its political action committees and the more than $41 million they've given to Congress and the White House, is it any wonder Israel is shielded from any shame?
>
> For more than 54 years the Israelis have committed acts that no other nation would dare get away with. But even here in America, where it is not yet illegal to publicly ask the wrong questions, any public figure that does so is subjected to smears, intimidation, and the attempted destruction of his career and reputation by Jewish organizations and by the very cooperative news media.[7]

But enough of quoting others. Let's look at the facts of Zionist control.

MEDIA: ABC, NBC, CBS, CNN, UPN, the *Washington Post*, the *New York Times*, the *Wall Street Journal*, the *New York Daily News*, *Time* magazine, *Newsweek*, *People* magazine, *US News and World Report*, and countless other media and Hollywood companies all have either a Zionist CEO, or a Zionist News President, or are owned by a media conglomerate which has a Zionist CEO.[8]

Have you ever noticed how Hollywood movies always seem to portray Germans and Arabs as bigoted fanatics or terrorists? Now you know why!

GOVERNMENT: AIPAC (the Israeli lobbying organization), and the ADL are the most feared political pressure groups in Washington DC.

Also carrying heavy political clout are well funded and well organized Zionist groups such as JINSA (Jewish Institute for National Security Affairs), ZOA (Zionist Organization of America), and AJC (American Jewish Congress.) By their own admission, these groups are capable of unseating Congressmen and Senators that do not carry out their requests.

AIPAC's method of operation is to withhold its money from any politician who strays from the pro-Israeli line, then to recruit an ambitious politician to run against their targeted Senator or Congressmen. AIPAC's awesome fund-raising machine and its media contacts are then placed at the disposal of their puppet candidate. The list of the political "scalps" that AIPAC has collected in this manner is impressive. It includes Senator William Fulbright and Senator Charles Percy, both former Chairmen of the Senate Foreign Relations committee, who tried to curb Israel's dominance over the US Senate.

Other AIPAC victims include Congressmen James Trafficant (ousted by a "scandal" after he spoke out against Israel), Congresswoman Cynthia McKinney, Congressman Earl Hilliard, and Congressman Paul Findley. The majority of Congressmen from both political parties receive large donations from AIPAC. Writing for the *Nation* magazine, journalist Michael Massing explains:

> AIPAC is widely regarded as the most powerful foreign-policy lobby in Washington. Its 60,000 members shower millions of dollars on hundreds of members of Congress on both sides of the aisle. Newspapers like the *New York Times* fear the Jewish lobby organizations as well. "It's very intimidating," said a correspondent at another large daily. "The pressure from these groups is relentless."[9]

PENTAGON: The Pentagon is under the control of a hard core group of Zionist moles led by the maniacal Richard Perle. The civilian Defense Policy Board actually wields more control over the military establishment than the Defense Secretary or the generals and admirals. A number of other Zionists serve on this Board, including Kissinger, Cohen, Schlessinger, Adelman, and Abrams, as well as non-Jewish members who have always supported Israel and the expansion of the "War on Terror."

The notoriously belligerent Perle, nicknamed the "The Prince of Darkness," is Chairman of the Defense Policy Board.[10] Perle is also a former member of the Board of Directors of the *Jerusalem Post* and serves on the Board of Directors of several Israeli companies. Shortly after 9-11, Perle helped organize a full page open letter to George Bush which appeared in the *New York Times*. Directed at his own boss, the letter urged Bush to finish off Saddam Hussein in a total war. Highly articulate and persuasive, Perle has also appeared on numerous TV shows as an "American" advocate for a total war on Iraq. Of course, not once did any of the talk show hosts ever mention Perle's deep Israeli connections.

The Undersecretary of Defense is Paul Wolfowitz, another Zionist zealot who lived in Israel as a teenager and has family living there now. Like Perle, Wolfowitz has appeared on many news shows, always banging the war drums against Iraq. At times his war-mongering borders on hysteria, such as this comment made on CNN: "Iraq is trying to develop weapons of mass destruction that would make September 11 pale by comparison."[11]

As with Perle, not once has a single talk show host mentioned Wolfowitz's deep Israeli connections as a possible motive for his desire to attack Iraq.

The Undersecretary of Defense Policy is Douglass Feith, a Zionist award winner whose law firm actually has offices in Israel. Feith has been serving Israel's interests in and out of government for about 20 years. During that time he has publicly urged three different presidents (Bush I, Clinton, and Bush II) to forcibly remove Saddam Hussein from power.

The Zionist Pentagon gang of Perle, Wolfowitz, and Feith represent three of the top four civilian leadership positions of America's armed forces. Even NASA is now under the control of a Zionist named Daniel Saul Goldin. Careerist scoundrels like Condoleezza Rice and Donald Rumsfeld are either under their influence or unwilling to oppose their drive for World War III. The Perle-Wolfowitz-Feith gang constitutes a fanatical, powerful and warmongering "government-within-a-government."

In league with these Zionist Pentagon conspirators are Orthodox Jewish Zionist and probable 2004 Presidential candidate, Senator Joseph Lieberman (D-CT), his partner in crime, Senator John McCain (R-AZ), and scores of other Zionist or Zionist-owned Senators, Congressmen, and media personalities. It is from this "behind-the-scenes" cabal that the curious obsession to attack Iraq emanates.

An Israeli journalist named Ari Shavit, commenting on Zionist influence over America while lamenting the harsh treatments that his government dishes out to the Palestinians, made the following observation in *Ha'aretz*, a leading Israeli journal:

> We believe with absolute certitude that now, with the White House and Senate in our hands along with the Pentagon and the *New York Times*, the lives [of Arabs] do not count as much as our own. Their blood does not count as much as our blood. We believe with absolute certitude that now, when we have AIPAC [the Israel lobby] and [Edgar] Bronfman and the Anti-Defamation League, we truly have the right to tell 400,000 people that in eight hours they must flee from their homes. And that we have the right to rain bombs on their villages and towns and populated areas. That we have the right to kill without any guilt.[12]

This only scratches the surface of Zionist power. We haven't even mentioned the powerful Zionist element that dominates finance (Greenspan, Soros, Rothschild, Goldman, Sachs, Schwab, Warburg etc.), publishing (Simon & Schuster, Newhouse Publications, etc.), and the academic world. With such awesome power to control and cover up events, is it any wonder why so many of America's journalists, intellectuals, and politicians are afraid to even talk about this issue?

Is it any wonder why President Bill Clinton would grovel before a Jewish audience at a $350 a plate dinner, and utter something as ridiculously pathetic as the following statement:

> The Israelis know that if the Iraqi or the Iranian army came across the Jordan River, I would personally grab a rifle, get in a ditch, and fight and die.[13]

It was very fitting that Bill Clinton should have made those comments before a Zionist women's charity called the Hadassah Foundation. Hadassah (also known as Esther) is the heroine of the Book of Esther in the Old Testament. This non-religious story tells of a scheme by Hadassah and her Uncle Mordecai to infiltrate and gain political influence over the Persian King Xerxes; influence which was then used to kill and destroy their anti-Jewish enemies.

I could go on at much greater length about Zionist power in banking, academia and book publishing, but I want to get back to the dancing Israelis. Have I made my point yet?

8

The Butcher Sharon

One more quick lesson needs to be covered before we climb into the time machine and fast-forward back to 9-11. If we don't cover this, you won't be able to fully understand the "big picture."

During the 1967 war, Israel occupied the Palestinian territories of the West Bank and Gaza. Thirty-five years have passed since that war ended, yet the Israeli army continues the humiliating occupation of those Palestinian areas. These areas are not part of the nation of Israel that was created in 1948 by the UN. What the Palestinian people are resisting today is not the 1948 confiscation of their land. They simply want the 1967 Occupation to end. It is this ongoing Occupation, not the 1948 creation of Israel, that fuels the conflict today.

Prior to the current outbreak of hostilities, the majority of the Israeli people also supported the end of Israel's occupation and oppression of these territories. They elected Yitzak Rabin as Prime Minister and Rabin made more strides than any of his predecessors toward achieving peace.

The 1990s were quiet years in Israel. Palestinian leader Yasser Arafat and Prime Minister Rabin appeared to have finally reached a peace deal with Bill Clinton acting as the mediator.

This did not sit well with the hard core Zionists who ultimately hope to expand Israel's borders even more. Hopes for a lasting peace deal were soon dealt a major setback when a flurry of five bullets was pumped into Prime Minister Rabin at close range as he was attending a 1995 Israeli peace rally.

It was not an Arab who killed Rabin. It was a Zionist fanatic named Yigal Amir. Amir was a law student at Israel's Bar-Ilan University. He later told investigators that he was acting upon God's orders and had no regrets for his actions.[1]

Amir, a bright young law student was willing to throw his life away in the service of the Zionist cause.

With Rabin dead, the Israelis soon reverted to their murderous policies. In April of 1996, the US-funded Israeli military shelled Qana, a UN refugee camp in southern Lebanon. As always, the pretext the Israelis used was that "terrorists" were hiding in the camps. But when the smoke had cleared, 100 helpless civilians (mainly women and children) were left dead and mutilated by the Israeli onslaught. UN peacekeepers who were overseeing the camp later expressed shock at the horror they witnessed.

Much of the world condemned Israel for Qana but the United States said nothing! We just kept writing the checks which funded this evil military machine. And we wonder why some Arabs hate us! The aftermath of the Qana massacre was captured on a UN soldier's video-camera. If the reader has the stomach for it, a graphic video can be viewed at: http://jerusalem.indymedia.org/news/2003/01/101620.php.

Rabin was dead but Clinton kept pressuring Israel to make a modest deal with Arafat. This is not to suggest that Clinton was an anti-Zionist in any way. To the contrary, Clinton's mild peace-for territory proposals were heavily slanted in Israel's favor, and Clinton's Cabinet was loaded with such prominent Zionists as Sandy Berger (National Security Advisor), Madeline Albright (Secretary of State), Robert Rubin (Secretary of Treasury) and William Cohen (Secretary of Defense). But in his self-serving and ego-maniacal quest to win a Nobel Peace prize (or simply to leave a lasting historical legacy for his presidency) Clinton pushed a bit too hard for the paranoid Zionists' comfort.

Two years after Rabin's murder, Zionist "neo-conservatives" (ex-Democrat Zionists who infiltrated and now also control the Republican Party) finished off the derailment of the peace process by weakening Bill Clinton. The impeachment of Bill Clinton during the Monica Lewinsky sex and perjury scandal had its origins in the behind-the-scenes manipulations of a prominent Zionist New York City socialite named Lucianne Goldberg.

It was Goldberg who played Linda Tripp like a fiddle by urging her to secretly tape record her private conversations with Monica Lewinsky. When the tapes became public, they revealed that Clinton had lied under oath in previous testimony given for a sexual harassment lawsuit which had been brought against him by Paula Jones. In a most unusual move, a prominent Democratic Senator then broke with his own President and Party and denounced Clinton's conduct as "immoral" on the floor of the Senate.

Although gullible Republicans were quick to praise this Senator for "putting principles ahead of his Party," the Senator had ulterior motives for wanting to weaken Clinton.

Who was this Senator who embarrassed his own Party's leader on the Senate floor? It was none other than the Orthodox Jew and arch-Zionist, Joe Lieberman![2]

Influential Zionist "neo-conservative" journalists including William Safire, William Kristol, Charles Krauthammer, and JJ Goldberg (Lucianne's son!) ignited the feeding frenzy against Clinton, who suddenly became so pre-occupied with surviving the scandal that he could longer focus on the Middle-East.

Republicans, who had no idea what forces were really at work, eagerly joined the lynch mob against a corrupt and suddenly vulnerable President who had always seemed untouchable, despite having previously engaged in far more serious criminal activity than "Monica-gate." First Lady Hilary Clinton publicly claimed that "a vast right wing conspiracy" was out to get her husband. She was essentially correct in her analysis, but her use of the vague term "right-wing conspiracy" wasn't exactly accurate. It was really a "Zionist wing conspiracy" aided by a bunch of Republican suckers who had other legitimate reasons to dislike a scumbag such as Bill Clinton. Of course, someone in Hilary's position wouldn't dare admit such a thing publicly. If she had, you can be sure she would never have been elected as a New York Senator in 2000!

When the sad saga had finally played itself out, Clinton was impeached and greatly weakened, America was disgraced, and poor manipulated Linda Tripp became the target of Clinton's vindictive wrath, nearly ending up in jail and eventually losing her job. The only winners were Lucianne Goldberg and the Israel Firsters who had paid Clinton back for daring to have Palestinian leader Yasser Arafat as an honored guest at the White House. The peace process seemed doomed.

At the head of the Israeli government today sits a brutal man who has been a guest of honor at George Bush's White House on a regular basis since he took office in October 2000. He was a close political ally of the terrorist-turned Prime Minister Menachem Begin. His name is Ariel Sharon. It was Sharon who, as Defense Minister in the early 80s, engineered the merciless destruction of the once beautiful Lebanese city of Beirut. His fanatical Zionist supporters in Israel refer to him as "Arik King," but the Arabs know him as a lifelong butcher, terrorist, and war criminal.

There was a time when Sharon was disgraced and his political career seemed to be over. The isolation of Ariel Sharon was the result a 1982 Palestinian massacre which Sharon engineered when he was Israel's Defense minister. It was the Israeli people themselves who forced Sharon to resign. Sharon took the heat for Prime Minister Begin.

Sharon's troops had blocked the exits from the Sabra and Shattila refugee camps while a Lebanese militia, allied with the Israeli military, went into the camps, slaughtered more than 1,500 unarmed Palestinian civilians and raped many women.[3] Although the Lebanese militia were the ones who did the actual killing, it was Ariel Sharon who controlled the militias and it was Sharon's soldiers who stood by and blocked the camp exits, deliberately allowing the slaughter to take place.

A survivor of the attack who had been raped and shot went to Belgium and initiated a war crimes case against Sharon. Several Lebanese militia leaders were summoned to testify against Sharon in late 2001/early 2002. Shortly before their testimony, three of them were suddenly killed by unknown gunmen and car bombs. Israel's Mossad of course denied any responsibility for the strange and untimely deaths of these three witnesses against Sharon.[4] If you believe that lie, I'll sell you the World Trade Center!

After nearly 20 years of political exile, Sharon made his comeback in October 2000 by initiating the third and final step of the Zionist peace-killing scheme (Steps 1 and 2 were the Rabin assassination and the Clinton-Monica scandal). Knowing full well how much the Palestinians hated him for his role in the 1982 massacres, Sharon and a small army of Israeli soldiers showed up at the Temple Mount, a site held sacred by both Muslims and Jews.[5]

This was a deliberate provocation. When the Muslims protested the Sharon provocation, the Israeli troops cracked down. Rocks were thrown and shots fired. In just a matter of minutes, years of peace and the Israeli-Arab peace effort had been finally undone by Mr. Sharon's bullying antics. When the fighting broke out, a frightened and propagandized Israeli population soon turned to a strong man for their protection—the very man who had deliberately instigated the violence in the first place! Ariel Sharon was elected Prime Minister. The stage was now set for a major war. The only missing ingredient was the "incident," the "Pearl Harbor" that would be needed to bring the US into the war on Israel's side.

True to form, Sharon has brutalized and terrorized the Palestinian civilian population under the pretext of "self-defense." Armed and funded by Israel's wholly owned US Congress and totally supported by a brainwashed American public that has been led to believe that Israel(!) is the poor defenseless victim, the Israeli war machine has bulldozed and bombed Arab homes at will, uprooted their olive tree crops, shot scores of children in the head, prevented ambulances from assisting the wounded, bombed hospitals, shot and killed foreign journalists, physicians and peace activists, held up pregnant women at checkpoints, terrorized priests and nuns and killed an alter boy at Bethlehem's Church of the Nativity, siphoned off drinking water from thirsty Palestinians to use for spas for newly-arrived Jewish settlers, beaten and tortured any Palestinian male who dares to resist the occupation, urinated and defecated in Arab homes (on the floor!), shot a 95-year-old woman to death, broadcast hard-core pornography into Arab homes after capturing Palestinian TV stations, planted booby traps which have killed children ... and so much more.

The terror is so shocking, many young Israeli soldiers who do have a conscience have left the military in protest and refuse to participate in the oppression. More than 400 soldiers signed an open-letter entitled "Courage to Refuse" in which they expose the lies about the war on Palestine as well as Sharon's brutality.[6] Some ex-soldiers have even been treated for psychological trauma caused by their guilt over the horrors they helped carry out against the Palestinians.

In the face of these atrocities, America's gutless politicians, corrupted clergy and lying journalists have remained silent. Against the US-financed Israeli war machine, the only weapons the outgunned and desperate Palestinians can retaliate with are sling shots and "suicide bombers." With every suicide bombing (some of which having the appearance of "frame-up jobs" carried out by unwitting Arab patsies), Sharon is able to falsely accuse Arafat, "justify" even more attacks, and grab more land.

The Zionist game plan is to ultimately drive all of the Palestinians out of the West Bank and Gaza, just as the Irgun massacres drove the Arabs out of Deir Yassin and so many other Arab villages. This scheme is known as "transfer." Standing in the way of such a bold Zionist act were three major obstacles:

The force of world opinion. Prior to 9-11, the Palestinian struggle against Israeli occupation had gained the sympathy of many people around the world.

The force of Israeli domestic opinion. Most Israelis wanted peace and were opposed to the 35-year occupation of Palestinian territories.

Saddam Hussein's oil rich Iraq, which had always been a champion of the cause of Palestinian self-determination and a militarily strong obstacle to Israel's expansionist ambitions.

How useful it would be for the Zionists if some "incident" were to happen which would suddenly turn American, Israeli, and world opinion against the Palestinians. How useful such an "incident" would be in ultimately dragging the US into a war against Israel's Arab and Muslim enemies, a war under whose noisy cover Palestine could be "ethnically cleansed" (transferred) once and for all.

If only a modern-day "Pearl Harbor" would happen to kick off such a chain of events, something big ... something unforgettable ... something so horrific and unthinkable, it would induce the American people into a boiling hatred for the Arabs/Muslims! It did happen ... on 9-11. Now you know why those five Israelis were "dancing, high-five-ing and celebrating."

9

Advance Warnings

The days and hours leading up to 9-11 were marked by a series of chilling warnings about impending terrorist plots involving hijacked commercial airplanes. It is worth mentioning at this point that months before 9-11, the US had already informed some of its allies of plans to go to war in Afghanistan. On June 26, 2001, *News Insight/India Reacts*, an Indian public affairs magazine, wrote:

> India and Iran will "facilitate" US and Russian plans for "limited military action" against the Taliban if the contemplated tough new economic sanctions don't bend Afghanistan's fundamentalist regime. Indian officials say that India and Iran will only play the role of "facilitator" while the US and Russia will combat the Taliban from the front with the help of two Central Asian countries, Tajikistan and Uzbekistan, to push Taliban lines back to the 1998 position 50 km away from Mazar-e-Sharief city in northern Afghanistan. Military action will be the last option though it now seems scarcely avoidable.[1]

The story of US military involvement in Afghanistan was reported months before 9-11 in respected Indian[2] and British[3] publications but it was never reported in the US media. With the military plans already in motion since at least June of 2001, all that was needed was for an "incident," a modern-day Pearl Harbor attack, to take place to justify the US going to "war against Terrorism" in Afghanistan.

As far back as 1998, a group of "neo-conservatives" known as "The Project for the New American Century" (PNAC) issued open letters to then President Bill Clinton and Republican House leaders calling for the removal of Saddam Hussein from power in Iraq. This was to be achieved by military force if necessary. Beyond Iraq, the "neo-cons" wanted the US to pursue a more aggressive policy throughout the Middle East.

Signatories to these letters included hard core Zionists Richard Perle, Paul Wolfowitz and William Kristol, as well as political hacks such as Donald Rumsfeld and Dick Cheney. Keep in mind that despite the presence of a few opportunistic gentiles in their ranks (Cheney, Rumsfeld, etc.) the movement known as "neo-conservatism" was founded and always dominated by influential Zionist intellectuals in both government and media (Kristol, Podhoretz, Decter, Goldberg, Abrams, Perle, Wolfowitz, Safire, Krauthammer, Feith, Adelman, Libby, Rosenthal, Wurmser, etc.).

Neo-conservative war-mongers from PNAC understood there was one very large obstacle standing in the way of their grand schemes for going to war against Iraq and other Arab nations. That obstacle was the force of American public opinion. The Zionist schemers openly stated that it might take a "New Pearl Harbor" to bring their dreams to their bloody fruition. ("New Pearl Harbor" is PNAC's own language, not this author's!)

A March 10, 2003 ABC *Nightline* report described the dilemma these neo-conservatives (i.e., Zionists and their stooges) faced. In a segment titled "The Plan: Were Neo-Conservatives 1998 Memos a Blueprint for War?" *Nightline* reported:

> Years before George W. Bush entered the White House, and years before the Sept. 11 attacks set the direction of his presidency, a group of influential neo-conservatives hatched a plan to get Saddam Hussein out of power.

> The group, the Project for the New American Century, or PNAC, was founded in 1997. Among its supporters were three Republican former officials who were sitting out the Democratic presidency of Bill Clinton: Donald Rumsfeld, Dick Cheney and Paul Wolfowitz.

In open letters to Clinton and GOP congressional leaders the next year, the group called for "the removal of Saddam Hussein's regime from power" and a shift toward a more assertive US policy in the Middle East, including the use of force if necessary to unseat Saddam.

And in a report just before the 2000 election that would bring Bush to power, the group predicted that the shift would come about slowly, unless there were "some catastrophic and catalyzing event, like a new Pearl Harbor." That event came on Sept. 11, 2001. By that time, Cheney was vice president, Rumsfeld was secretary of defense, and Wolfowitz his deputy at the Pentagon.[4]

Adding further intrigue to PNAC's chilling advance mention of a "new Pearl Harbor" were some of the actual advance warnings brought to light in the aftermath of 9-11. The *London Daily Telegraph* reported on September 16, 2001:

> The *Telegraph* has learned that two senior experts with Mossad, the Israeli military intelligence service, were sent to Washington in August to alert the FBI and CIA to the existence of a cell of as many as 200 terrorists said to be preparing a big operation. They had no specific information about what was being planned but linked the plot to Osama Bin Laden and told American officials there were strong grounds for suspecting Iraqi involvement.[5]

Do you smell a "false flag" operation in the works? How is it possible that the Mossad knew of the existence of these 200 terrorists but could not name or locate a single one of them for us? And how convenient for Israel that Saddam Hussein should be "in cahoots" with Osama Bin Laden, despite the fact that Bin Laden and Hussein hate each other! (Bin Laden is a Muslim Fundamentalist who views the secular Hussein as a westernized idolater.)

The *Frankfurter Allgemeine Zeitung*, (FAZ) one of Germany's most respected newspapers, quoted German intelligence sources who said that the Echelon electronic spy network gave US and Israeli intelligence agencies several warnings that suicidal hijack attacks were being planned against US targets.[6]

Echelon is capable of monitoring all electronic communication in the world. Utilizing 120 satellites, Echelon is designed to suck up enormous amounts of data by using keyword search techniques to sift through the data.[7]

The *San Francisco Chronicle* reported on September 12 that San Francisco Mayor and former California Assembly Speaker Willie Brown were advised eight hours before the attacks that they should be careful about flying on 9-11.[8] According to a Pacifica Radio report on May 17, 2002, the warning to Mayor Brown came from National Security Advisor and fellow San Franciscan, Condoleezza Rice.

In its September 24, 2001 issue, *Newsweek* broke this startling revelation:

> Three weeks ago there was another warning that a terrorist strike might be imminent ... On September 10, *Newsweek* has learned, a group of top Pentagon officials suddenly cancelled travel plans for the next morning, apparently because of security concerns.[9]

Could these unnamed "top Pentagon officials" have been some of the Zionist directors of the Defense Policy Board mentioned earlier? If these Pentagon officials were scared enough not to fly, then why didn't the Pentagon place the Air Force on full alert? How could they have been so slow to react to 9-11 when they already knew there was a threat?

On September 27, the *Washington Post* reported that two workers of the Israeli company messaging Odigo (with offices also in New York) received instant message warnings just two hours before the attacks. Here's an excerpt from the *Post*:

> Officials at instant-messaging firm Odigo confirmed today that two employees received text messages warning of an attack on the World Trade Center two hours before terrorists crashed planes into the New York landmarks.[10]

Soon after the attacks, Odigo employees informed the management of the electronic message they had received. Israeli security services were contacted and the FBI was informed. Nothing has been heard about this event since. I think it is safe to say that "Islamic terrorists" would not have been considerate enough to send detailed e-mail warnings to some obscure Israeli office workers.

10

The September 11 Dance Party

Let us review what we have learned. We have clearly established that Zionists played a key role in steering the US into two World Wars. We have clearly established that Zionists do not care if Americans (or others) are killed to further their goals. We have clearly established that Zionists have a record of attacking Americans in order to frame Arabs. We have established that the Zionists are capable of acts of unspeakable brutality and genocide.

We have established that US politicians fear the Zionist Mafia and defy them at their own peril. We have learned that warnings of a suicidal hijacking plot were issued to several people. And most important of all, we have clearly established that the Zionists have the capacity to make these amazing stories suddenly disappear from their controlled media even after the stories initially penetrated their own screens.

Having established these precedents, we can now easily deduce that the reason why those five dancing Israeli agents who celebrated the 9-11 attacks were so happy is because they knew that Americans would now become unconditional supporters of their "Israeli ally" and fanatical haters of Muslims, Palestinians, and other Arabs.

On the day of the attacks, former Israeli Prime Minister Benjamin Netanyahu was asked what the attack would mean for US-Israeli relations. His quick reply was: "It's very good ... (then he caught himself and added) ... Well, it's not good, but it will generate immediate sympathy for Israel."[1]

Not only did the attacks generate immediate sympathy for Israel; they also generated immediate and intense hatred for Arabs and Muslims. In the days following 9-11, there were numerous cases of violent attacks (in some cases murderous) against innocent Muslims. Incited to hatred by the Zionist media, violent and ignorant American lemmings even attacked (and in one case killed) Indian Hindus!

The five Israeli army veterans (Mossad) made quite a public spectacle. Police had received several calls from angry New Jersey residents claiming that "Middle-Eastern" men with a white van were celebrating and filming the disaster. Witnesses saw them celebrating at Liberty State Park after the initial impact.

Later on, other witnesses saw them celebrating on a roof in Weehawken, and still more witnesses later saw them celebrating in a Jersey City parking lot. But the one call in particular that led authorities to actually close down all New York bridges and tunnels came from a mysterious anonymous person. This mystery caller told the 9-11 dispatcher that a group of Palestinians were mixing a bomb inside a white van headed for the Holland Tunnel. Here's the transcript from NBC News:

Dispatcher: Jersey City police.

Caller: Yes, we have a white van, 2 or 3 guys in there, they look like Palestinians* and going around a building.

Caller: There's a mini-van heading toward the Holland tunnel, I see the guy by Newark Airport mixing some junk and he has those sheikh uniform.

Dispatcher: He has what?

Caller: He's dressed like an Arab.[2]

[*Why would this mystery caller specifically say that these "Arabs" were Palestinians"? How would he know that? Palestinians usually dress in western style clothes, not "sheikh uniforms."]

Based on that phone call, police then issued a "Be-on-the-Lookout" alert for a white mini-van heading for the city's bridges and tunnels from New Jersey. When a van fitting that exact description was stopped just before crossing into New York, the suspicious "Middle-Easterners" were apprehended. Imagine the surprise of the police officers when these terror suspects turned out to be Israelis!

According to ABC's *20/20*, when the van belonging to the cheering Israelis was stopped by the police, the first words out of the driver's (Sivan Kurzberg) lying mouth were:

"We are Israelis. We are not your problem. Your problems are our problems. The Palestinians are your problem."[3]

The police and FBI field agents really became suspicious when they found box cutters (the same items that the hijackers supposedly used), $4700 cash stuffed in a sock, and foreign passports. Police also told the Bergen Record that bomb sniffing dogs were brought to the van and they reacted as if they had smelled explosives.[4] Israeli Army Radio later reported that a white van with a bomb was stopped as it approached the George Washington Bridge. Here's what the *Jerusalem Post* reported on September 12, 2001:

> American security services overnight stopped a car bomb on the George Washington Bridge ... The van, packed with explosives, was stopped on an approach ramp to the bridge. Authorities suspect the terrorists intended to blow up the main crossing between New Jersey and New York, Army Radio reported."[5] *Jerusalem Post*, September 12, 2001, "Car Bomb found on George Washington Bridge."

The Israeli Army Radio would have known about such a plot because Israeli Army veterans (Mossad) were the plotters! Of course, Army Radio did not reveal the true ethnicity of the suspects. The listeners are left to assume that the detained bombers were Arabs. What's really intriguing is that ABC's *20/20*,[6] the *New York Post*,[7] and the *New Jersey Bergen Record*,[8] all clearly and unambiguously reported that a white van with Israelis was intercepted on a ramp near Route 3, which leads directly to the Lincoln Tunnel.

But the Israeli Army Radio & *Jerusalem Post* [see footnote 5], Israeli National News [*Arutz Sheva*][9] and *Yediot America*[10] all reported, just as clearly and unambiguously, that a white van with Israelis was stopped on a ramp leading to the George Washington Bridge, which is several miles north of the Lincoln Tunnel.

It appears as if there may actually have been two white vans involved, one stopped on each crossing. This would not only explain the conflicting reports as to the actual location of the arrests, but would also explain how so many credible eye-witnesses all saw celebrating "Middle-Easterners" in a white van in so many different locations. It also explains why the *New York Post* and Steve Gordon (lawyer for the five Israelis) originally described how three Israelis were arrested but later increased the total to five. Perhaps one van was meant to drop off a bomb while the other was meant to pick up the first set of drivers while re-crossing back into New Jersey?

If a van was to be used as a parked time-bomb on the George Washington Bridge, then certainly the drivers would need to have a "get-away van" to pick them up and escape. And notice how the van (or vans) stayed away from the third major crossing—the Holland Tunnel—which was where the police had originally been directed to by that anti-Palestinian 9-11 "mystery caller." A classic misdirection play.

From there, the story becomes even more suspicious. The Israelis worked for a Weehawken moving company known as Urban Moving Systems. An American employee of Urban Moving Systems told the *Bergen Record* that a majority of his co-workers were Israelis and they were all joking about the attacks. The employee, who declined to give his name said: "I was in tears. These guys were joking and that bothered me."[11]

A few days after the attacks, Urban Moving System's Israeli owner, Dominick Suter, dropped his business and fled the country for Israel. He was in such a hurry to flee America that some of Urban Moving System's customers were left with their furniture stranded in storage facilities.[12] It was later confirmed that the five Israeli army veterans were in fact Mossad agents.[13] They were held in custody for several months before being quietly released.

Some of the movers had been kept in solitary confinement for 40 days.[14]

It doesn't take Sherlock Holmes to put together the dots of the dancing Israeli Mossad agents and logically deduce the truth. Here is the most logical scenario:

1. The Israeli "movers" cheered the 9-11 attacks to celebrate the successful accomplishment of the greatest spy operation ever pulled off in history.
2. One of them, or an accomplice, then calls a 9-11 police dispatcher to report Palestinian bomb-makers in a white van headed for the Holland Tunnel.
3. Having thus pre-framed the Palestinians with this phone call, the Israeli bombers then head for the George Washington Bridge instead, where they will drop off their time-bomb van and escape with Urban Moving accomplices.
4. But the police react very wisely and proactively by closing off ALL bridges and tunnels instead of just the Holland Tunnel. This move inadvertently foils the Israelis' misdirection play and leads to their own capture and 40-day torture.
5. To cover up this story, the US Justice Department rounds up over 1000 Arabs for minor immigration violations and places them in New York area jails. The Israelis therefore become less conspicuous as the government and media can now claim that the Israelis were just immigration violators caught in the same dragnet as many other Arabs.
6. After several months, FBI and Justice Department "higher-ups" are able to gradually push aside the local FBI agents and free the Israelis quietly.

The Zionist controlled media ignored this Israeli connection. Immediately following the 9-11 attacks, the media was filled with stories linking the attacks to Bin Laden. TV talking-heads, "experts" and scribblers of every stripe spoon-fed a gullible American public a steady diet of the most outrageous propaganda imaginable. We were told that the reason Bin Laden attacked the US was because he hates our "freedom" and "democracy." The Muslims were "medieval" and they wanted to destroy us because they envied our wealth, were still bitter about the Crusades, and were offended by Britney Spears shaking her tits and ass all over the place!

Amazingly, millions of media-addicted Americans actually swallowed this fallacious fecal matter about the "Clash of Civilizations!" But Bin Laden strongly denied any role in the attacks and suggested that Zionists orchestrated the 9-11 attacks. The BBC published Bin Laden's statement of denial in which he said:

> I was not involved in the September 11 attacks in the United States nor did I have knowledge of the attacks. There exists a government within a government within the United States. The United States should try to trace the perpetrators of these attacks within itself; to the people who want to make the present century a century of conflict between Islam and Christianity. That secret government must be asked as to who carried out the attacks ... The American system is totally in control of the Jews, whose first priority is Israel, not the United States.[15]

You never heard that quote on your nightly newscast did you?! Although the *New York Times* did publish parts of that interview, the above quote was censored by Zionist Arthur Sulzberger's elitist propaganda sheet. To date, the only shred of "evidence" to be uncovered against Bin Laden was a highly suspicious, barely audible, fuzzy amateur video that the Zionist-dominated Pentagon just happened to find "lying around" in Afghanistan. How very convenient! Though there is no evidence, be it hard or circumstantial, to link the Al-Qaeda "terrorist network" to these acts of terror, there is in fact a mountain of evidence, both hard and circumstantial, which suggests that the Zionist Mafia has been very busy framing Arabs for terror plots against America.

11

Who Was Really Flying Those Planes?

Hours after the 9-11 attacks, authorities began to find clues conveniently left for them to stumble upon. The *Boston Globe* reported that a copy of the Koran, instructions on how to fly a commercial airplane, and a fuel consumption calculator were found in a pair of bags meant for one of the hijacked flights that left from Logan.[1]

Authorities also received a "tip" about a suspicious white car left behind at Boston's Logan Airport. An Arabic-language flight training manual was found inside the car.[2] How fortunate for investigators that the hijackers forgot to take their Koran and Arab flight manuals with them! Within a few days, all "19 hijackers" were "identified" and their faces were plastered all over our television screens.

Then, like a script from a corny "B" spy movie, the official story gets even more ridiculous. The passport of the supposed "ringleader" Mohammed Atta, somehow managed to survive the explosion, inferno and smoldering collapse to be oh-so-conveniently "found" just a few blocks away from the World Trade Center![3] Days later, another "hijacker" passport belonging to Ziad Jarrah was found at the Flight 93 crash site in Pennsylvania.[4] Why would these hijackers take passports with them on internal domestic flights anyway?

It is obvious that this "evidence" was planted by individuals wishing to direct the blame toward Osama Bin Laden. How is it possible that Arab students who had never flown an airplane could take a simulator course and then fly jumbo jets with the skill and precision of "top-gun" pilots? It is not possible and the fact is, the true identities of the 9-11 hijackers remains a mystery. In the days following the disclosure of the "hijackers'" names and faces, no less than 7 of the Arab individuals named came forward to protest their obvious innocence.[5]

That's right! Seven of the nineteen "hijackers" are alive and well. They were victims of identity theft, some of whom had had their passports stolen. They were interviewed by several news organizations including the *Telegraph* of England. Here's an excerpt from David Harrison's *Telegraph* story titled: "Revealed: The Men With Stolen Identities":

> Their names were flashed around the world as suicide hijackers who carried out the attacks on America. But yesterday four innocent men told how their identities had been stolen . . .
>
> The men—all from Saudi Arabia—spoke of their shock at being mistakenly named by the FBI as suicide terrorists. None of the four was in the United States on September 11 and all are alive in their home country.
>
> The *Telegraph* obtained the first interviews with the men since they learnt that they were on the FBI's list of hijackers who died in the crashes in New York, Washington and Pennsylvania.
>
> All four said that they were "outraged" to be identified as terrorists. One has never been to America and another is a Saudi Airlines pilot who was on a training course in Tunisia at the time of the attacks. Saudi Airlines said it was considering legal action against the FBI for seriously damaging its reputation and that of its pilots.[6]

The story of these identity thefts was also briefly reported by ABC[7] and BBC (England).[8] The FBI does not deny this. Nobody denies this fact because it is easily verifiable. Instead, the US media and government just ignore this inconvenient little fact and keep right on repeating the monstrous lie that the hijacker identities are known and that 15 of them were Saudis.

CNN revealed that FBI director Robert Mueller openly admitted that some of the identities of the 9-11 hijackers are in question due to identity theft. Here's what CNN reported on September 21:

> FBI Director Robert Mueller has acknowledged that some of those behind last week's terror attacks may have stolen the identification of other people, and, according to at least one security expert, it may have been "relatively easy" based on their level of sophistication.[9]

The *Washington Post*, under the headline "Some Hijacker Identities Remain Uncertain" reported:

> FBI officials said yesterday that some of the 19 terrorists who carried out last week's assault on New York and Washington may have stolen the identities of other people, and their real names may remain unknown. Saudi government officials also said yesterday that they have determined that at least two of the terrorists used the names of living, law-abiding Saudi citizens. Other hijackers may have faked their identities as well, they said.

> FBI Director Robert Mueller said Friday that the bureau had "a fairly high level of confidence" that the hijacker names released by the FBI were not aliases. But one senior official said that "there may be some question with regard to the identity of at least some of them."

> The uncertainty highlights how difficult it may be to ever identify some of the hijackers who participated in the deadliest act of violence on American soil. Most of the hijackers' bodies were obliterated in the fiery crashes. "This operation had tremendous security, and using false names would have been part of it," said John Martin, retired chief of the Justice Department's internal security section.

"The hijackers themselves may not have known the others' true names."[10]

This opens up a whole Pandora's box of unanswered questions. First and foremost: why would Osama Bin laden, the Saudi Arabian caveman, steal identities? To cover his tracks you say? OK. Next question: Why would a Saudi Arabian, attempting to cover his tracks, steal the identities of... FELLOW SAUDI ARABIANS??? What would be the point? Why go through the trouble of stealing identities that would only point back to you? Why not steal Greek identities, or Brazilian identities, or Turkish ones?

A much more logical conclusion is that non-Arabs stole these identities as part of a "false flag" operation designed to point the blame at Arabs, and Saudi Arabs in particular.

What kind of a corrupt character is FBI boss Mueller? He initially admitted that false identities were involved with 9-11, but then he allowed the media to keep naming these innocent, and alive, Arabs as the hijackers. Why doesn't he correct them? More on the slimy Mr. Mueller later on!

Now I'm really going to rock your faith in the false religion of 9-11. In February of 2000, Indian intelligence officials detained 11 members of what they thought was an Al-Qaeda hijacking conspiracy. It was then discovered that these 11 "Muslim preachers" were all Israeli nationals! India's leading weekly magazine, *The Week*, reported:

> On January 12 Indian intelligence officials in Calcutta detained 11 foreign nationals for interrogation before they were to board a Dhaka-bound Bangladesh Biman flight. They were detained on the suspicion of being hijackers. "But we realized that they were *tablighis* (Islamic preachers), so we let them go," said an Intelligence official.

> The eleven had Israeli passports but were believed to be Afghan nationals who had spent a while in Iran ... Indian intelligence officials, too, were surprised by the nationality profile of the eleven. "They say that they have been on *tabliqhi* (preaching Islam) in India for two months. But they

are Israeli nationals from the West Bank," said a Central Intelligence official.

He claimed that Tel Aviv "exerted considerable pressure" on Delhi to secure their release. "It appeared that they could be working for a sensitive organization in Israel and were on a mission to Bangladesh, the official said."[11]

What on earth were these 11 Israeli agents doing trying to impersonate Muslim hijackers? Infiltrating? Perhaps. Framing? More likely. But the important precedent to understand is this: Israeli agents were once caught red-handed impersonating Muslim hijackers!

This event becomes even more mind boggling when we learn that it was Indian Intelligence that helped the US to so quickly identify the "19 hijackers"! On April 3, 2002, *Express India*, quoting the *Press Trust* of India, revealed:

> Washington, April 3: Indian intelligence agencies helped the US to identify the hijackers who carried out the deadly September 11 terrorist attacks in New York and Washington, a media report said here on Wednesday.[12]

Did you catch that? The Indian intelligence officials who were duped into mistaking Israeli agents for Al-Qaeda hijackers back in 2000—were the very same clowns telling the FBI who it was that hijacked the 9-11 planes! Keep in mind that Indian intelligence has an extremely close working relationship with Israel's Mossad because both governments hate the Muslim nation of Pakistan.[13]

Now about Mohamed Atta, you know, the so-called "ring leader." There are a number of inconsistencies with that story as well. Like some of the seven hijackers known to be still alive, Atta also had his passport stolen in 1999 (the same passport that miraculously survived the WTC explosion and collapse?) making him an easy mark for an identity theft.[14] Atta was known to all as a shy, timid and sheltered young man who was uncomfortable with women.[15] The five-foot-seven 150-pound architecture student was such a "goody two shoes," some of his university acquaintances in

Germany refrained from drinking or cursing in front of him. How this gentle, non-political mamma's boy from a good Egyptian family suddenly transformed himself into the vodka drinking, go-go girl chasing terrorist animal described by the media, has to rank as the greatest personality change since another classic work of fiction, *Dr. Jekyll and Mr. Hyde.*

Atta, or someone using Atta's identity, had enrolled in a Florida flight school in 2001 and then broke off his training, conveniently telling his instructor he was leaving for Boston. In an October 2001 interview with an ABC affiliate in Florida, flight school president Rudi Dekkers said his course does not qualify pilots to fly commercial jumbo jets.[16] He also described Atta as "an asshole."[17] Part of the reason for Dekker's dislike for Atta stems from a highly unusual incident that occurred at the beginning of the course. Here's the exchange between ABC producer, Quentin McDermott and Dekkers:

McDermott: Why do you say Atta was an asshole?

Dekkers: Well, when Atta was here and I saw his face on several occasions in the building, then I know that they're regular students and then I try to talk to them, it's kind of a PR—where are you from . . . I tried to communicate with him. I found out from my people that he lived in Hamburg and he spoke German, so one of the days that I saw him—I speak German myself—I'm a Dutch citizen, and I started in the morning telling him in German, "Good morning. How are you? How do you like the coffee? Are you happy here?" And he looked at me with cold eyes, didn't react at all and walked away. That was one of my first meetings I had.[18]

This is eerily similar to the way in which Zacharias Moussaoui (the so-called "20th hijacker") became "belligerent" when his Minnesota flight instructor tried to speak to him in French (his first language), at the beginning of that course. The *Minnesota Star Tribune* reported on December 21, 2001:

Moussaoui first raised eyebrows when, during a simple introductory exchange, he said he was from France, but then didn't seem to understand when the instructor spoke

French to him. Moussaoui then became belligerent and evasive about his background, (Congressman) Oberstar and other sources said. In addition, he seemed inept in basic flying procedure, while seeking expensive training on an advanced commercial jet simulator.[19]

It truly is an amazing twist of fate that both Atta and Moussaoui both had American flight instructors who spoke German and French respectively. Even the great Mossad could not have foreseen such a coincidence! The real Atta would have been able to respond to his instructor's German small talk, and the real Moussaoui would have been able to respond to his instructor's French small talk. Atta just walked away and Moussaoui threw a fit! Neither responded because neither could. They were imposters, whose faces were probably disguised by a make-up artist. Their mission was to frame the two innocent Arabs who were probably targeted by the Mossad at random.

The imposter was able to create a new Atta by using Atta's stolen passport from 1999—the same passport that floated safely to the ground with a few burnt edges on 9-11. These strange inconsistencies tend to give support to Mohammed Atta's father's claim that he spoke over the phone with his son on September 12, the day after the attacks.[20]

Could a group of professionals have abducted and killed the real Atta in the days following the 9-11 attacks? Mossad agents, posing as "art students" were arrested after conducting some type of operation in Hollywood, Florida, the same small town where "Atta" stayed![21] So what happened to the real Mohammed Atta? To quote his grief-stricken father: "Ask Mossad!"

So who, if not the "19 Arabs" was on those planes? That's the million dollar question! There are a number of alternative scenarios. Could some Israelis have been fanatical enough to have volunteered for such a suicide mission? Odd as that may sound at first, it is not out of the realm of possibility. The fact is, hard-core Zionist extremists have proven themselves to be every bit as fanatical (perhaps even more so), than Arab extremists.

A nation that can produce thousands of bloodthirsty, Purim-celebrating, Zionist extremists, Irgun war criminals, Mossad terrorists who blow up occupied buildings, assassins who kill Israeli

Prime Ministers in full view of policemen, and crazed killers who have carried out sickening massacres of Arab women and children; would surely be capable of recruiting a few fanatics willing to sacrifice for "the cause." This theory becomes even more plausible when we consider that only the pilots would have needed to know that the planes were on a suicide mission.

Still don't think Israel is capable of producing suicidal terrorists? Have you already forgotten the case of Dr. Baruch Goldstein? Goldstein was a New York doctor and father of four who resettled in Israel. On February 25, 1994, Goldstein walked into a crowded Arab mosque in the occupied West Bank. With hundreds of Muslims kneeling in silent prayer, Goldstein sealed off the exit and opened fire with a rapid-firing assault rifle, killing 29 and wounding many more. Goldstein was finally stopped and killed when the frenzied crowd overpowered him. With as many as 800 worshippers packed into the mosque, Goldstein surely could not have been expecting to come out alive. This was clearly a suicide attack. And what did Goldstein's mother have to say about her son's suicide attack? The *Boston Globe* revealed:

> The mother of Baruch Goldstein, the Jewish settler who massacred about 40 Palestinians in a Hebron mosque a week ago, says she is proud of her son. "I always thought to myself, 'When would someone get up and do such a thing?' And in the end, my son did it," Miriam Goldstein told the *Shishi* newspaper.[22]

It gets even more sickening than that. Baruch Goldstein has become a folk hero among many of the crazed, side-locked, machine gun-toting settlers who have encroached upon the West Bank. They have turned Goldstein's gravesite into a memorial and set up a website to honor his murderous deed! Look what these fanatics posted on the Goldstein memorial website:

> Over the years, the grave has become a site of pilgrimage. Numerous people from all over the world come to pray and honor his (Baruch's) memory.[23]

The exact date on which Dr. Goldstein chose to carry out his one man genocide-suicide has a special significance for hard-core, fundamentalist Zionists. That year (1994), the Jewish holiday of Purim (see the "Book of Esther" in the Old Testament) fell on February 25. Purim celebrates the mass killing of the Jews' ancient Persian enemies. The heroine of the story is named Hadassah. Hadassah and her Uncle Mordecai gain influence over King Xerxes and use that influence to save the Jews from the persecution of the hated vizier named Haman.

Hadassah and Mordecai persuade Xerxes to issue a decree of extermination against Haman and the "anti-Semites" of Persia. Under the direction of Uncle Mordecai and the blessing of his puppet King Xerxes, the Jews of Persia proceed to carry out a mass killing of Persians. Chapter 9 of the "Book of Esther" tells the bloody story:

> All the people were seized with fear of the Jews. Moreover, all the officials of the provinces, the satraps, governors, and royal procurators supported the Jews for fear of Mordecai: for Mordecai was powerful in the royal palace and he was continually growing in power ... In Susa, the Jews killed and destroyed 500 men.

> The Jews struck down all their enemies with the sword, killing and destroying them: they did to their enemies as they pleased ... When the number of those killed was reported to the king, he said to Queen Esther: "You shall be granted whatever you ask." So Esther said, "If it pleases your majesty, let the Jews be permitted again tomorrow to act according to today's decree, and let the ten sons of Haman be hanged on gibbets." So the ten sons of Haman were hanged, and the Jews mustered again ... and killed 300 men in Susa. The other Jews who dwelt in the royal provinces also mustered ... they killed 75,000 of their foes.

We later learn that Mordecai decrees that Hadassah's Persian genocide campaign should be celebrated each year by a festival. The Jewish holiday of Purim is in fact celebrated to this very day. Dr. Goldstein celebrated Hadassah's brutality on Purim 1994, literally, by murdering 29 Muslims as they prayed in their own mosque!

One can't help but notice the ominous similarities between the Purim story and today's events. Purim 2002: starring Saddam Hussein as Haman, Richard Perle as Uncle Mordecai, George Bush as Puppet-King Xerxes, and Hadassah Lieberman as . . . Hadassah! That's right, Senator (and future president?) Joe Lieberman's wife (future First Lady?) is actually named Hadassah! One has to wonder if some of Dr. Goldstein's "Purim-aniac" admirers were flying those planes on 9-11.

Then there is the case of Irv Rubin, another dedicated family man and former head of the radical Jewish Defense League. Rubin and an associate were arrested in California in December of 2001 after they were caught plotting to blow up a Muslim mosque and the office of a US Congressman of Arab descent. Rubin later committed suicide in jail by slitting his own throat.[24]

One interesting side note here which may or may not be of any significance: One of the two Israelis who died aboard the hijacked planes was Daniel Lewin—who was aboard the first plane that crashed into the Twin Towers. *Ha'aretz* News Service of Israel revealed that Lewin was a one-time officer in the Israeli Defense Forces' elite *Sayeret Matkal* commando unit.[25]

Another possibility is that some other group of "patsies" was recruited for the operation. Perhaps some anarchists, or some left-over Marxists who thought they were going to bring down western capitalism. Or perhaps the hijackers were another group of angry Arab patsies who weren't even aware of who their true handlers really were or what the broader strategic aim of the mission actually was.

In the dark world of covert operations, agents are often kept ignorant of who is actually orchestrating the show, and nobody does this better than the Mossad!

Admittedly, these scenarios are speculative, but one thing that is not speculative is this: the hijackers were not the same 19 men whose faces were shown on our TV screens.

12

Who Provided Protective Cover for the 9-11 Operation?

On October 26, 1999, the famous golfer, Payne Stewart boarded a private Learjet in Florida and left for Texas. Shortly after takeoff, Stewart's jet veered sharply off course and began heading northwest. All contact with air controllers was lost.

Within 15 minutes of having gone off course, US fighter jets had already intercepted the jet. Everyone on board was likely dead due to depressurization. These fighter jets were dispatched by NORAD, the branch of the US air force whose job it is to monitor and defend US airspace 24 hours a day. NORAD works closely with NASA and maintains a huge array of land-based radar systems.

NORAD's fighter jets are on alert 24 hours a day so they can respond to any crisis. The jets escorted the doomed airplane until another group of Air National Guard jets took over the escort mission. Finally, Stewart's jet ran out of fuel and crashed in South Dakota. The quick reaction time and military precision with which NORAD intercepted and escorted Stewart's jet was impressive, and exactly what one would have expected from the greatest military and technological power in world history.[1]

But on 9-11, the same NORAD which had so effortlessly intercepted Stewart's jet in 1999, was nowhere to be found during that two-hour period between the first planes going off course and the last one crashing in a Pennsylvania field. How is it possible that the airspace between Boston and Washington DC, an area which contains the political and economic heart of the nation, was left completely defenseless?

The second plane to hit in New York had flown off course without communication for 40 minutes. On its way to New York, it actually flew within a few miles of McGuire Air Force base in New Jersey, after the first tower had already been hit! And how is it possible that Washington DC was left undefended (long after the New York attacks) when Andrews Air Force base is within car driving distance? The air force jets which did finally arrive were too late. Was this due to NORAD's incompetence, or was the order to scramble the fighter jets deliberately delayed, so the terror attacks could take place?

Given NORAD's impressive performance in the 1999 Payne Stewart disaster, this would suggest that someone high up in the Air Force establishment may have issued stand down orders to some of our Air Force bases. Remember, the Pentagon's Defense Policy Board is headed by Zionist Richard Perle and his gang of war-mongering lackeys.[2] Civilians on this board wield the power to promote career-minded Generals and Admirals. Is it really that hard to believe that a highly placed military leader could have collaborated with the true 9-11 planners?

Could NASA (which works hand in hand with NORAD) whose director is Zionist Daniel Saul Goldin, somehow be connected to NORAD's sudden "negligence" on 9-11?

What makes the Air Force's slow response even more outrageous, puzzling and suspicious is the previously mentioned revelation in a *Newsweek* article that several Pentagon leaders (Defense Policy Board? Perle? Feith? Wolfowitz?) canceled flight plans for September 11 due to security concerns.[3] There were other warning signals also, which we reviewed earlier.

In light of all these warnings, why weren't NORAD and its armada of fighters placed on an even higher alert than they already were? There is only one logical answer to these questions: Certain Pentagon leaders were "in on it." Some high level Intelligence officials around the world have come to the same conclusion.

General Hamid Gul, a former Director of Pakistani Intelligence appears to have hit the nail on the head with his analysis:

> The attacks against New York and Washington were Israeli engineered ... The attacks started at 8:45, and four flights are diverted from their assigned air space and no Air Force fighter jets scramble until 10:00. Radars are jammed, transponders fail and no IFF—friend or foe identification—challenge. In Pakistan, if there is no response to an IFF, jets are instantly scrambled. This was clearly an inside job. Will this also be hushed up in the investigation, like the Kennedy assassination?[4]

The German newspaper, *Der Tagesspiegel*, interviewed Andreas von Bülow, the former head of the parliamentary commission that oversees Germany's secret services:

> "The planning of the attacks was technically and organizationally a master achievement—to hijack four huge airplanes within a few minutes and within one hour, to drive them into their targets, with complicated flight maneuvers," said von Bülow in the *Tagesspiegel* interview. "This is unthinkable, without years of support from state intelligence services.

> "For 60 decisive minutes, the military and intelligence agencies let the fighter planes stay on the ground; 48 hours later, however, the F.B.I. presented a list of suicide attackers. Within ten days, it emerged that seven of them were still alive."

This led the interviewer to call Von Bülow "a conspiracy theorist." To which Von Bülow responded:

> "Yeah, yeah. That's the ridicule from those who prefer to follow the official, politically correct line," Von Bülow responded. "Even investigative journalists are fed propaganda and disinformation. Anyone who doubts the official line is called crazy."

> "With the help of the horrifying attacks, the Western mass democracies are being subjected to brainwashing. The

enemy image of anti-communism doesn't work anymore; it is to be replaced by peoples of Islamic belief. They are accused of having given birth to suicidal terrorism." [5]

Both Hamid Gul and Andreas Von Bülow accuse Israel's Mossad and elements within the US of being responsible for 9-11. These charges drew this response from George Bush, who said in a speech before the United Nations in November of 2001:

Let us never tolerate outrageous conspiracy theories concerning the attacks of September the Eleventh—malicious lies that attempt to shift the blame away from the terrorists themselves, away from the guilty. [6]

If the "conspiracy theories" surrounding 9-11 are so "outrageous," why would the President of the United States even bother to bring up the subject in front of a highly educated audience consisting of the world's top political leaders? Would a Nobel Prize winning scientist go out of his way to condemn "outrageous" flat earth theories during a speech before the world's top scientists? Would the US Surgeon General, speaking before the American Medical Association, go out of his way to condemn the "outrageous" and long since discredited practice of deliberately bleeding dying patients? It seems to this writer that Bush protests too much.

Not surprisingly, Bush's main speechwriter during 2001, Daniel Frum, is a hard core Zionist.[7] Bush's Press Secretary, Ari Fleischer, is another Israel Firster who actually referred to Ariel Sharon as "a Man of Peace"![8] Not only do these Zionists tell Bush what to do, but they apparently tell him what to say (or read) too. Given Bush's diminished intellectual capacities (likely exacerbated by 20 years of drunkenness), this too is not surprising.

Bush, or should I say, Frum & Fleischer, understandably have no tolerance for "outrageous conspiracy theories," but too many unanswered questions still arise.

Surely the masterminds of the 9-11 operation would have taken the time to learn something about US air defense procedures. They would therefore have realized that hitting New York City with jets hijacked from Boston would have been difficult. New York is about 30 minutes away by airplane and jumbo jets fly very slowly when compared to US fighter jets that crack the sound barrier. Even with a 15–20 minute head start, NORAD's jets could have easily intercepted them, especially the second plane, which took a longer route to New York and flew way off course for 40 minutes.

Why choose Boston's airport and jeopardize the success of the operation? Wouldn't it be safer to just hijack planes from New York's Kennedy or La Guardia Airports? Or even Newark, which is just across the river. Any plane hijacked from either of those three busy airports would have been unstoppable. Even a plane from Philadelphia's Airport would have been much closer to the target than far away Boston.

The planners were no dummies. They must have counted on receiving protective cover and a window of opportunity by someone high up at US Air command. Why else choose Boston? In addition to the protection that the planners were to receive from certain Air Force elements, there is another plausible theory for choosing Boston's Logan Airport as well as United and American Airlines planes. It should be noted that the firm which provides security at Boston's Logan Airport and also Newark Airport, and also works extensively with United and American Airlines, is a company called Huntleigh USA.[9]

Claiming that Huntleigh USA's airport security was grossly negligent on 9-11, family members of some of the victims are suing Huntleigh.[10] Huntleigh USA had been acquired by ICTS International in 1999. ICTS is controlled by two Israelis: Ezra Harel and Menachem Atzmon.[11]

In short, security at Boston's Logan airport was handled (or mishandled) by an Israeli controlled company. Is there a connection here? Could agents have been infiltrated into Logan Airport under Israeli owned Huntleigh's cover? It's quite possible. In the days following the 9-11 attacks, Israeli security professionals began aggressively marketing themselves in order to gain more airport security jobs.[12] Americans should be grateful to have such wonderful allies who care about our airport security so much!

Could some of the failure of our defense systems be attributed to a cyber attack from computer hackers? Our defense and intelligence systems are very dependent upon technology. A well coordinated attack on these systems may also have contributed to our inability to expose and prevent the attacks. There is one group that has the capability to attack our military computer systems.

In July of 1999, *Ha'aretz* (Israel) ran a story headlined: "Hackers Using Israeli Net Site to Strike at Pentagon." *Ha'aretz* reported:

> An Israeli Internet site is being used by international computer hackers as a base for electronic attacks on US government and military computer systems, according to Pentagon officials who were quoted in a *Washington Times* report yesterday.
>
> According to the *Times*, the real danger to US national security is the threat posed by foreign intelligence services or governments that could launch electronic warfare against the United States.[13]

And look what the US Department of Justice wrote in this 1998 press release:

> WASHINGTON, DC ... The Department of Justice, in conjunction with the FBI, the Air Force Office of Special Investigation, the National Aeronautic and Space Administration and the Naval Criminal Investigative Service, announced today that the Israeli National Police arrested Ehud Tenebaum, an Israeli citizen, for illegally accessing computers belonging to the Israeli and United States governments, as well as hundreds of other commercial and educational systems in the United States and elsewhere.[14]

No doubt about it. Covert elements in Israel have been targeting the US military's defense systems for some time now. This could very well have been yet another instrument played during the great orchestrated concert of 9-11.

13

The Curious Collapse of the Twin Towers and World Trade Center Number 7

The government/media-approved version of events insists that the fires in the World Trade Center burned so hot, they caused steel supports to melt and buckle, thus triggering a total collapse of the towers and also the perfectly methodical collapse of WTC Number 7 (which was never even hit by a plane!). Amazingly, this hasty theory was stated (and repeated endlessly) as an absolute fact from the very moment the first building started collapsing! This is a strange theory for a number of reasons:

1. The world class architects who designed the World Trade Center designed it to withstand the direct impact and fuel fire of a commercial airline crash. Aaron Swirsky, one of the architects of the WTC described the collapse as "incredible" and "unbelievable."[1] Lee Robertson, the project's structural engineer said: "I designed it for a 707 to hit it. The Boeing 707 has a fuel capacity comparable to the 767."[2]

2. The history of high-rise building fires provides not a single case of a building collapsing due to steel beams melting from a fire.

3. The total collapse of WTC 1, WTC 2, AND WTC 7 (a massive 47-story skyscraper which was never even hit by a plane) was all perfectly symmetrical and methodical. The three straight-down collapses were all identical in appearance to well-engineered, controlled implosions that are known as "smooth waves" in the demolition field. [To see a rarely shown CBS video of the perfect collapse of WTC 7, on the Internet, go to www.whatreallyhappened.com/wtc7.html.]

This video, originally shown live on CBS, will make your jaw drop! WTC 7 is shown completely intact with fire barely even visible. Dan Rather had already informed his viewers that "CBS has learned" that the building was expected to collapse. Shortly afterward, the bottom suddenly dropped out from underneath it. Within 2–3 seconds the entire 47-story building had suddenly disappeared into a perfect and total straight-down collapse! A demolition company could not have done it better.

It was claimed that diesel fuel which was stored in the building was somehow ignited and caused the collapse. Now that we know that all one has to do to bring a skyscraper straight down is set a fuel fire in it, the well-trained experts who work for demolition companies should all be out of a job by now.

Even a layperson without a background in explosives engineering should be able to see this . . . and many specialists in both explosives and structural engineering also made this observation and commented on these inconsistencies.

After the WTC collapse, the Vice President of New Mexico Tech, Van Romero, gave an interview to the *Albuquerque Journal*. Romero, an explosives and demolitions expert, stated that he believed the WTC collapse was too methodical and that explosive devices must have been placed in key points of both buildings. Romero said:

> It would be difficult for something from the plane to trigger an event like that. It could have been a relatively small amount of explosives placed in strategic points. One of the things that terrorists are noted for is a diversionary attack and a secondary device.[3]

In that same interview, Romero revealed that he was in Washington DC when the attacks took place. He and a colleague were there to discuss defense research programs for New Mexico Tech. A few days after his interview, Romero abruptly changed his opinion and told the *Albuquerque Journal* that he no longer believed that bombs brought down the towers.[4] Romero, who relies upon the Zionist-occupied Pentagon for funding, had suddenly flip-flopped and joined the "melted steel" theorists.

The days when buildings could only be brought down by stacks of dynamite or huge kegs of explosives are long gone. Today's plastic explosives, such as C-4, are so powerful, just a small handful of the stuff set off by remote control, can easily split a thick steel beam and pulverize concrete. The manufacture and distribution of C-4 is regulated so tightly, its very use would indicate the presence of a national intelligence service such as the CIA or Mossad.

Is it really that difficult to believe these buildings could have been imploded? If you stop to think about it for a moment, rigging key points of WTC 1, 2, and 7 with small amounts of C-4 would actually have been the easiest part of the whole operation—much easier to pull off than recruiting and training suicide hijackers, commandeering four planes within minutes of each other, evading US air defenses, and slamming the planes into their targets with military precision. Compared to that, affixing a wad of C-4 on a few support columns would have been a piece of cake!

More than just my own common sense and Romero's expert opinion support the belief that the towers were imploded from within. Several witnesses and survivors reported hearing bombs going off inside the World Trade Center. Louie Cacchioli is a firefighter with Engine 47 in Harlem, New York. Cacchioli told *People* magazine the following:

> I was taking firefighters up in the elevator to the 24th floor to get in position to evacuate workers. On the last trip up a bomb went off. We think there were bombs set in the building.[5]

This whole controversy between the "melted steel" and detonation scenarios is one that could easily be resolved. All we have to do is dig up the main steel support beams and examine each and every one of them. If an explosive device caused the steel to fail, there will be tell-tale indications for the engineers to see. But if it was intense heat that caused the steel to "melt" or "buckle," there will be tell-tale signs of that as well. All we have to do to put an end to this controversy is to closely examine the steel. Right? Don't hold your breath. That's never going to happen. Thanks in large part to *Time* Magazine's "Person of the Year 2001," New York Mayor Rudy Giuliani, the steel beams were quickly recycled before investigators were even given a chance to look at them! A media darling and lifelong supporter of Israel, Saint Rudy Giuliani made sure all of the "smoking gun" evidence was destroyed—and right quick too. Much of the steel was recycled in America, but an additional seventy thousand tons of WTC steel were sold to Metals Management—a New York company with a Jewish (Zionist?) president, Alan Ratner. Ratner then turned around and shipped the unexamined steel to China and India for recycling![6]

China Radio International's English Edition also reported:

New York's Metals Management is among the firms taking steel from the huge project to clear Ground Zero. The company says it has bought 70,000 tons of scrap from the ruined twin towers. Some of the scrap has been shipped across the Pacific to Asian, including China and India. Among the consignments of scrap are the "very dense" steel girders from Ground Zero, which could finally yield 250,000 to 400,000 tons of scrap for recycling.[7]

Imagine that! The largest criminal investigation in history, the most spectacular and educational event in the history of building fires, and the engineers weren't even permitted to see the most important evidence of all—the steel! This is akin to an archeologist discovering a complete skeleton of a previously unknown species of dinosaur, a species larger than a Brontosaurus, with teeth longer than a T-Rex, and a wingspan wider than a Pterodactyl's, and then having the government take it away and sell the bones to a necklace factory! It's simply unthinkable!

During the entire time that Saint Rudy the Recycler and Ratner the Rat were destroying evidence, many of the most respected engineers in the country openly complained not only about the recycling, but also about the Federal government's suffocating control of their investigation. On December 25, 2001, the *New York Times* ran a story about the frustrations of some of the engineers who were called in to study the cause of the collapse:

> Interviews with a handful of members of the team, which includes some of the nation's most respected engineers, also uncovered complaints that they had at various times been shackled with bureaucratic restrictions that prevented them from interviewing witnesses, examining the disaster site and requesting crucial information like recorded distress calls to the police and fire departments ...[8]

They made their concerns known publicly. Bill Manning, editor of the 125-year-old *Fire Engineering* magazine, noticed a strange difference between the WTC investigation and other major fire investigations in New York City's past. Manning wrote:

> Did they throw away the locked doors from the Triangle Shirtwaist fire? Did they throw away the gas can used at the Happy Land social club fire? That's what they're doing at the World Trade Center. The destruction and removal of evidence must stop immediately.[9]

One investigator told the *New York Times*:

> "This is almost the dream team of engineers in the country working on this, and our hands are tied," said one team member who asked not to be identified. Members have been threatened with dismissal for speaking to the press. "FEMA is controlling everything," the team member said.[10]

Dr. Frederick W. Mowrer from the Fire Engineering department at the University of Maryland told the *New York Times*: "I find the speed with which important evidence has been removed and recycled to be appalling."[11]

Finally, the *Times* story made this interesting little revelation describing how Recycling Rudy, that ubiquitous fiend for publicity, suddenly became media shy:

> Officials in the mayor's office declined to reply to written and oral requests for comment over a three-day period about who decided to recycle the steel and the concern that the decision might be handicapping the investigation.[12]

It is a very odd form of science that the government and some of its house scientists practice these days. The government and media render a hasty verdict, then the scientists and engineers (who may be quite knowledgeable in their respective fields yet totally ignorant of geo-political realities) are asked to fill in the details. This is not science!

Without a shred of physical evidence, these modern-day alchemists have been able to "prove" their theory that it was fire that caused the three towers to collapse. This is a classic case of scientists (some of them well meaning, some of them deceitful) ignoring the basic scientific method by blindly accepting a prejudiced conclusion first, and then manipulating the data (either consciously or subconsciously) to fit their pre-determined, pseudo-scientific delusion. We must always remember that even the most highly trained scientist is still a human being, handicapped with the same psychological complexes and weaknesses that afflict the rest of us mere mortals.

And so you see, this "melted steel" scenario appears to be yet another monstrous lie. Why else would the "melted steel" have been destroyed in such a hurried manner? Ask Rudy.

14

The Miracle of Passover

It wasn't just Americans who were murdered on 9-11. Nearly 500 foreign-born nationals from over 70 different nations were killed in the World Trade Center.[1] As a center of world trade and finance this is not surprising. It is also commonly known that many Israelis work in the field of international trade and finance. The laws of probability dictate that among the nearly 500 dead foreign nationals, from over 70 different nations, there should have been a considerable number of Israelis. But the number of Israeli dead was suspiciously low, especially when we consider the report published in the September 12 *Jerusalem Post*, that the Israeli embassy in America was bombarded on 9-11 with calls from 4000 worried Israeli families.[2]

George Bush had told the US Congress that he also mourned the deaths of foreign citizens including "more than 130 Israelis."[3] But Bush was either misinformed by his Zionist speechwriter David Frum, or he was deliberately lying. The actual number of Israeli workers killed in the WTC was far less than 130. It was far less than 100. It was far less than 50. It was far less than 25. It was far less than 10. According to the *New York Times*, it was ... zero![4]

One Israeli was killed aboard each of the two flights that crashed into the WTC (an odd coincidence in and of itself) and one was killed while visiting on business. No regular Israel worker was actually killed in the WTC. That's right! Zero Israeli workers lost their lives in the WTC while citizens from over 70 different nations, including such powerhouses of world trade and finance as Granada, Bermuda, Ireland, and the Philippines, all lost people in the WTC. Here's the *Times* excerpt from September 22, 2001:

> ... the city had somehow received reports of many Israelis feared missing at the site, and President Bush in his address to the country on Thursday night mentioned that about 130 Israelis had died in the attacks. But Friday, Alon Pinkas, Israel's consul general here, said that lists of the missing included reports from people who had called in because, for instance, relatives in New York had not returned their phone calls from Israel.
>
> There were, in fact, only three Israelis who had been confirmed as dead: two on the planes and another who had been visiting the towers on business and who was identified and buried.[5]

We learned earlier about the employees of the Israeli instant messaging company Odigo, who were anonymously informed of the attacks two hours before they took place.[6] Even more intriguing than the Odigo warnings was the narrow escape of 200 employees of an Israeli government-run company called Zim Israel Navigational. With over 80 vessels, Zim Navigational is the ninth largest shipping company in the world. Just one week before 9-11, Zim Navigational moved out of its World Trade Center offices with over 200 workers.[7, 8] Company spokesperson Dan Nadler said: "When we watched the pictures, we felt so lucky. Our entire US operations were run out of the 16th floor."[9, 10]

Zim moved to Virginia. Nadler added that the aim of the sudden move "was to save on rent."[11, 12] Somehow the claim that a major global shipping firm, backed up by government money, needed to save a few bucks on rent lacks credibility. And oh, what perfect timing!

So who tipped off Zim? Who tipped off Odigo? Who tipped off those Pentagon officials? Who tipped off those Israeli workers in New York? Can we safely assume it wasn't Osama bin Laden from a cave in Afghanistan?

15

Framing Bin Laden

Within minutes after the attacks, a parade of politicians and "terrorism experts" appeared on every TV channel, all claiming that the attacks were the work of Osama bin Laden. A traumatized American public swallowed it all hook, line, and sinker, just like the real perpetrators knew we would. The Bush administration claimed it had evidence linking Bin Laden to the attacks which it would release to the public in a matter of days. They never did. Just like they never provided any evidence that Al-Qaeda blew up the US embassies in Africa in 1997.

The entire case against Osama Bin Laden was based on nothing but the repeated claim that he was the culprit for the embassy bombings and for 9-11. The entire case against Bin Laden was a mass brainwash job from the very start.

The US placed demands on the Taliban government of Afghanistan to turn Bin Laden over to the US or face an attack. We established earlier that US military action had already been planned since June.[1,2]

The Taliban offered to turn Bin Laden over to a neutral party if the US provided any evidence to them that he had anything to do with the 1997 US African embassy bombings or the 9-11 attacks. The evidence was never presented to the Taliban for two reasons:

1. There never was any evidence, not even circumstantial.
2. The war to replace the Taliban with a US puppet government was already in motion. The 9-11 attacks served as the perfect

excuse or "incident," the "new Pearl Harbor" needed to win the support of the American people and kick off the war.

Three months after the attacks, and with the bombing of Afghani peasants in full swing, the US had still not provided one shred of evidence to link Bin Laden and his Al-Qaeda "terrorist network" to 9-11. People in foreign countries were beginning to ask questions. Then one day, the Pentagon claimed that some unnamed source found a video tape in Afghanistan. The Bush gang began dropping hints in the media that this video showed Osama bin Laden bragging and admitting his role in the attacks.

How convenient! And how improbable. The "mastermind" of 9-11, who was so brilliant that he pulled off 9-11 without being detected, was careless enough to leave a "confession video" lying around to be discovered by the US!

The video was shown on the news with English subtitles. Bin Laden's voice was so faint and incoherent, even viewers in Arab nations had to rely on the Pentagon's translated subtitles! An obedient American (Zionist) news media accepted the Pentagon story and translation without question. A few Arab media whores were even trotted out to vouch for the tape's authenticity. Aha! This is the "smoking gun" they assured us. But this too is another vicious lie.

On December 20, 2001, the German TV show, *Monitor* (the "*60 Minutes*" of Germany) found the translation of the "confession" video to be not only "inaccurate," but even "manipulative."[3] Dr. Abdel El M. Husseini and Professor Gernot Rotter made an independent translation and accused the White House translators of "writing a lot of things that they wanted to hear but cannot be heard on the tape no matter how many times you listen to it."[4]

Even more compelling than the revelations of the European press are the actual images of the "confession video." Every photo previously taken of Osama bin Laden shows gaunt facial features and a long thin nose. The Pentagon video of Bin Laden clearly shows a man with full facial features and a wide nose. Examine the pictures side-by-side for yourself if you don't believe it. The differences in facial features will jump right out at you.[5]

Would the Pentagon leadership be capable of such deception? Why not?! They were capable of allowing 9-11 to happen, weren't they? The Pentagon itself has even admitted the existence of a special department, The Office of Strategic Influence (OSI) established for the purpose of planting false stories in the media in order to carry out strategic objectives. [The very pro-Zionist and very pro-war *New York Times* broke a story in February 2002 which revealed that the Pentagon has plans to deliberately provide false stories to the press as part of an effort to influence policy. The Pentagon set up the Office of Strategic Influence (OSI) for this purpose. A Zionist Air Force General named Simon P. Worden was chosen to head this criminal effort.[6] Worden's boss is Douglass Feith, another dedicated Zionist who serves as Undersecretary of Defense for Policy.]

How dedicated a Zionist is Douglass Feith? The Zionist Organization of America (ZOA) honored Feith and his father at an award dinner in 1999. Following is the ZOA's 1997 press release about this event:

> This year's honorees will be Dalck Feith and Douglas J. Feith, the noted Jewish philanthropists and pro-Israel activists. Dalck Feith will receive the ZOA's special Centennial Award at the dinner, for his lifetime of service to Israel and the Jewish people. His son, Douglas J. Feith, the former Deputy Assistant Secretary of Defense, will receive the prestigious Louis D. Brandeis Award at the dinner. [Google users, enter: feith zionist organization award][7]

There you have it: the Zionist Air Force General who runs the Pentagon's media disinformation department, reports directly to a Zionist Pentagon boss, who was a recipient of the "prestigious" Louis Brandeis Award. Brandeis, a former Supreme Court judge, was one of the key Zionist powerbrokers who helped influence Woodrow Wilson into joining World War I as part of the Zionist-British Balfour deal we learned about earlier. Remember this the next time some new "video" or "tape" that seems to implicate Muslims surfaces out of nowhere.

The most mind boggling, ridiculous and yet scariest part of this story is that General Worden later went on to tell a US

Congressional committee hearing on asteroids that an asteroid might one day hit Pakistan and be mistaken for a nuclear bomb, thus triggering a nuclear war between Muslim Pakistan and pro-Israeli India! Behold this bit of brazen bovine excrement from admitted liar Worden, courtesy of CNN:

> "An asteroid 5 to 10 meters in diameter exploded in June over the Mediterranean Sea, releasing as much energy as the atomic bomb dropped on Hiroshima in World War II," Worden told the House Committee on Science. "Imagine that the bright flash accompanied by a damaging shock wave had occurred over India or Pakistan."[8]

Worden noted that at the time the two countries were near the brink of war and either could have mistaken it for a surprise attack. Wouldn't that be convenient for the Pakistan-hating Zionists! After 9-11, I wouldn't put anything past them.

Two years have passed since the 9-11 attacks, and the FBI has not uncovered any Al-Qaeda cells in the United States, nor has it found any paper trail. The *London Times* reported:

> Thousands of FBI agents have rounded up more than 1,300 suspects across America since September 11, but they have failed to find a single Al-Qaeda cell operating in the United States ... Tom Ridge, Director of Homeland Security could not explain why none had been caught.[9]

In April 2002, FBI director Robert Mueller—the same Robert Mueller who admitted that several hijacker identities were in doubt due to identity thefts—made this stunning announcement: "In our investigation, we have not uncovered a single piece of paper—either here or in the treasure trove of information that has turned up in Afghanistan and elsewhere—that mentioned any aspect of the September 11 plot."[10]

Predictably, Directors Ridge and Mueller attribute this total lack of evidence to the skill of the Al-Qaeda "terrorist network." If you've read this far you should know better. The reason the US has been unable to uncover a shred of evidence to link Al-Qaeda to 9-11 is because ... Al-Qaeda didn't do it!

16

Hundreds of Mossad Agents Caught Running Wild in America!

We have discussed at length about the five celebrating Israeli "movers" (Mossad agents) who were arrested and placed in solitary confinement for weeks after they were spotted in a white van suspected of attempting to blow up the George Washington Bridge. We also reviewed how the Israeli owner of Urban Moving Systems, Dominick Suter, then suddenly abandoned his "moving company" and fled for Israel on September 14. But still more Israeli "movers" and other Israelis' actions raised serious suspicions. Even more suspicious is how they are always quietly released and deported.

In October of 2001, three more Israeli "movers" were stopped in Plymouth, PA because of their suspicious behavior. These "movers" were seen dumping furniture near a restaurant dumpster! When the restaurant manager approached the driver, a "Middle Eastern" man later identified as Moshe Elmakias fled the scene.[1] The manager made note of the truck's sign which read "Moving Systems Incorporated" and called the police. When the police spotted the truck, two other Israelis, Ayelet Reisler and Ron Katar, began acting suspiciously.[2]

The Plymouth police searched the truck and found a video. The Israelis were taken into custody and the video tape was played at the police station. The video revealed footage of Chicago with zoomed-in shots of the Sears Tower.[3]

The police quickly alerted the FBI and it was also discovered that the Israelis' travel logs and paper work were phony.[4] In addition, they were unable to provide a name and telephone number for the customer they claimed to have been working for.

These Israelis were up to some sort of dirty business, and you can be sure it had nothing to do with moving furniture. They may have had a dark sense of humor. The Israeli spies' "moving company" actually contained the word MOSSAD embedded in its name: "Moving Systems Incorporated: MOving SyStems IncorporAteD ... MOSSAD."

On October 10, 2001, CNN made a brief mention of a foiled terrorist bomb plot in the Mexican Parliament building. They promised to bring any further developments of this story to their viewers, but the incident was never heard of again in America. However, the story appeared in bold headlines on the front page of the major Mexican newspapers[5] and was also posted on the official website of the Mexican Justice Department.[6]

Two terror suspects were apprehended in the Mexican Chamber of Deputies. Caught red-handed, they had in their possession a high powered gun, nine hand grenades, and C-4 plastic explosives (great stuff for demolishing buildings!).[7] Within days, this blockbuster story not only disappeared from the Mexican press, but the Israelis were quietly released and deported. The two terrorists were Salvador Gerson Sunke and Sar ben Zui. Can you guess what their ethnicity was? Sunke was a Mexican Jew and Zui was a colonel with the Israeli special forces [MOSSAD].[8]

The story in El Diario de Mexico also revealed that the Zionist terrorists were carrying fake Pakistani passports. Can you say "false flag operation?" The probable motive of this particular botched terrorist operation was to involve oil rich Mexico in the "War on Terrorism." (The War on Israel's enemies would be a more accurate description.)

Mexico is no military power, but the psychological trauma of an "Arab" attack on Mexico would surely have induced Mexico to provide unlimited cheap oil to her American "protector." With cheap oil flowing to America at low prices from Mexico, the US could better afford to break off relations with the oil rich Arab states, particularly Saudi Arabia. That's why the planners chose 15 Saudi identities to steal for the 9-11 operation.

Many Mexicans expressed shock at the release of the two Israelis. But when you learn that Mexico's Secretary of Foreign Relations is a Zionist named Jorge Gutman, it is not surprising. The Zionist tentacles reach even into Mexico! *La Voz de Aztlan* (Mexican-American news service), in its excellent investigative report revealed:

> *La Voz de Aztlan* has learned that the Israeli Embassy used heavy handed measures to have the two Israelis released. Very high level emergency meetings took place between Mexican Secretary of Foreign Relations Jorge Gutman, General Macedo de la Concha and a top Ariel Sharon envoy who flew to Mexico City especially for that purpose. Elías Luf of the Israeli Embassy worked night and day and their official spokeswoman Hila Engelhart went into high gear after many hours of complete silence. What went on during those high level meetings no one knows, but many in Mexico are in disbelief at their release.[9]

In November 2001, six more suspicious Israelis were detained in an unspecified mid-eastern state. They had in their possession box cutters, oil pipeline plans, and nuclear power plant plans.[10] The local police called in the Feds and Immigration officials took over the scene. They released the men without calling the FBI. The *Jerusalem Post* ran this story under the headline, "FBI Suspects Israelis of Nuclear Terrorism."[11]

The *Miami Herald*[12] and the *Times* of London[13] also carried this amazing story that stated the FBI officials' fury that these Israeli terror suspects with nuclear power plant plans were set free by INS officials. Of course, the corruption-riddled FBI would only have caved in to Zionist pressure from the Justice Department's Criminal Division boss, Michael Chertoff, and also from the ADL's "partner," FBI boss Robert Mueller—who would no doubt have found a way to eventually release those Israeli terror suspects anyway.

In December 2001, the *Los Angeles Times* published the story of how two Jewish terrorists were arrested by the FBI for plotting to blow up the office of US Congressman of Arab descent, Darrell Issa (R-CA), and a California mosque.[14] Irv Rubin and Earl Kruger of the Jewish Defense League (JDL) were charged with conspiracy to destroy a building by means of explosives. This story got brief national coverage but then quickly disappeared.

In May 2002, yet another moving van was pulled over in Oak Harbor, Washington near the Whidbey Island Naval Air Station. Fox News reported the van was pulled over for speeding shortly after midnight. The passengers told the police they were delivering furniture, but because it was so late at night, the police weren't buying the story. A bomb sniffing dog was brought in and the dog detected the presence of TNT and RDX plastic explosives in the truck (great stuff for demolishing buildings!). Both Fox News[15] and *Ha'aretz* of Israel reported that the two "movers" were Israelis.[16]

In December 2002, Ariel Sharon made the amazing claim that Al-Qaeda agents were operating inside of Israel. But when Palestinian authorities apprehended the suspects, they turned out to be Palestinian traitors impersonating Al-Qaeda agents for the MOSSAD!

From the *Sydney Morning Herald* of Australia:

> Palestinian security forces have arrested a group of Palestinians for collaborating with Israel and posing as operatives of Osama Bin Laden's Al-Qaeda terrorist network, a senior official said yesterday ... The arrests come two days after Israeli Prime Minister Ariel Sharon charged Al-Qaeda militants were operating in Gaza and in Lebanon.

> It was considered a surprise because the Gaza Strip is virtually sealed off by Israeli troops. The hardline Israeli leader also charged other members of the terror group were cooperating with Lebanon's Shi'ite militia Hizbollah.[17]

If Sharon weren't so dangerous, one could almost be amused by his antics.

According to Fox news, throughout late 2000 and 2001, a total of 200 Israeli spies were arrested.[18] It was the largest spy ring to ever be uncovered in the history of the United States. The *Washington Post* also reported that some of these Israelis were arrested in connection with the 9-11 investigation.[19] Carl Cameron of Fox News Channel did an excellent four-part, nationally televised series of investigations into this blockbuster scandal, but Fox pulled the investigative series after Zionist groups complained to Fox executives. Fox even went so far as to remove the written transcripts of the series from its website! In its place was posted a chilling, Orwellian message which reads: "This story no longer exists."[20]

Fortunately for the sake of history, the Fox transcripts were copied onto too many other websites and all four parts are available for your review. [See footnotes.]

The Fox series and other mainstream news media sources revealed that many of these Israelis were army veterans with electronics and explosives expertise. Many of them failed lie detector tests. FBI agents told Fox that some of their past investigations were compromised because suspects had been tipped off by Israeli wiretapping specialists. It was discovered that Israeli companies such as Comverse and Amdocs have the capability to tap American telephones (great for blackmailing all those wife-cheating politicians, especially when we consider that some of the female Israelis who were arrested are said to have been quite attractive).

FBI agents also told Fox they believed the Israelis had advance knowledge of the 9-11 attacks (which certainly would explain why no Israelis died in the WTC). Still another US official informed Fox that some of the detained Israelis actually had links to 9-11, but he refused to describe the nature of those links. The FBI official told Fox's Carl Cameron:

"Evidence linking these Israelis to 9-11 is classified. I cannot tell you about the evidence that has been gathered. It is classified information."[21]

Then there was that small army of Israeli "art students" who were arrested for trying to sneak into secured US Federal buildings and staking out 36 Department of Defense sites. Some of these suspicious "art students" even showed up at the homes of Federal employees.[22] Ron Hatchett, a Department of Defense analyst, told Channel 11, KHOU News in Houston that he believed the "art students" were gathering intelligence for future attacks. Here's an excerpt from the October 1, 2001 KHOU investigative report by Anna Werner:

> Could federal buildings in Houston and other cities be under surveillance by foreign groups? That's what some experts are asking after federal law enforcement and security officials—nationally and in Houston—described for the 11 News Defenders a curious pattern of behavior by a group of people claiming to be Israeli art students.
>
> Hatchett says they could be doing what he would be doing if he were a terrorist, sizing up the situation: "We need to know what are the entrances to this particular building. We need to know what are the surveillance cameras that are operating. We need to know how many guards are at this operation, when do they take breaks?" Says Hatchett: "This is not a bunch of kids selling artwork."
>
> A former Defense Department analyst, Hatchett believes groups may be gathering intelligence for possible future attacks. "Some organization, thinking in terms of a potential retaliation against the US government could be scouting out potential targets and ... looking for targets that would be vulnerable."
>
> And a source tells the Defenders of another federal memo, stating that besides Houston and Dallas, the same thing has happened at sites in New York, Florida and six other states, and even more worrisome, at 36 sensitive Department of Defense sites. "One defense site you can explain," says Hatchett, "well that was just a serendipitous. Thirty-six? That's a pattern."[23]

A Federal memo stated that these "art students" may have had ties to an "Islamic terror group." More likely, they were the "Islamic terror group"!

Remember the bombing of the King David Hotel in 1946, and how the "Arab terrorists" were actually Irgun terrorists? Remember the Zionist terrorists caught in Mexico with Arab passports? Remember the official motto of the Mossad: "By Way of Deception Thou Shalt Do War"? Are you getting the picture? Can you say "false flag operations"?

In a follow-up report a few days later, KHOU Channel 11 revealed that Dallas was also targeted:

> 11 News reported how people claiming to be "Israeli art students" might be trying to sneak into federal buildings and defense sites, and even doing surveillance. And at least one expert said he thought it could all be preparation for an attack. Well, now federal sources say they are not ruling out that all of this could be connected with the hijackings on September 11, because of events in another Texas city.
>
> In Dallas, the so-called students hit early this year at the city's FBI building, the Drug Enforcement Administration and at the Earle Cabell Federal building, where guards found one student wandering the halls with a floor plan of the building.
>
> So the Dallas INS went on the alert, finding and arresting 15 people in March. Thirteen claimed to be Israelis and two are professed Colombians. But according to sources, once again their passports were phony. And another federal source says some of those arrested also appeared to have lists of federal employees and their home addresses.
>
> All 15 "students" have now been deported. Now, since our first story ran Sunday night, some viewers called who said that they've been visited by people who claim to be Israeli students selling art.[24]

Absolutely mind boggling! Why were Israeli explosives experts, posing as "art students" seen "wandering the halls" of US Federal buildings? Why were Israeli army vets, armed with explosives and detonators, "wandering the halls" of the Mexican Congress? Why were Israeli "movers" caught in vans with explosives residue? Might some of these shady characters have once also "wandered the halls" of the World Trade Center prior to 9-11? Or "wandered the halls" of the doomed US embassies in Africa in 1997? Or "wandered the halls" of the doomed tourist resort in Bali, Indonesia?

Why aren't *60 Minutes, Nightline, 20/20* and the rest of the Zionist media aggressively pursuing the story behind these "hall-wandering" Israeli "art students" and "movers" with 1/1,000th the zeal that they pursued Martha Stewart over allegations of insider trading (who cares?), or 1/10,000th the zeal that they pursued the Catholic Church over an occasional pedophile priest, or 1/100,000th the zeal that they pursue the Muslim bogeyman on a daily, nay, hourly basis? Something smells rotten here!

One would think these intriguing mysteries would have great TV audience appeal, especially in light of the fact that the Oklahoma Federal building was blown up in 1995 by the since-executed Timothy McVeigh (dead men tell no tales), and a "John Doe # 2" of "Middle-Eastern appearance" who was never tracked down or pursued despite numerous eye-witness accounts and despite an FBI All Points Bulletin which clearly described him as such. McVeigh may have planted the truck bomb, but the partial "smooth wave" collapse of the building again indicates that explosives were planted on the inside.

It's interesting to note that the group which was falsely accused of (and hurt the most by) the Oklahoma bombing was the American militia movement, a loosely knit coalition of armed anti-Zionist patriots. The ensuing outrage over the bombing decimated militia membership and fund raising nationwide, and totally broke the back of this emerging anti-Zionist movement. Abe Foxman and his crowd hated the militias almost as much as they hate Muslims. Here's what Dishonest Abe had to say about the militia bogeyman shortly after the 1995 terrorist attack:

> As long as there are people willing to actively buy into the incendiary, paranoid propaganda of extremist militia

leaders, we must take them seriously and remain alert to the threats they pose … The tools of today's technology are being utilized to promote their conspiratorial, anti-government, anti-gun control, and anti-Semitic message.[25]

"Paranoid," "extremist," "anti-Semitic" … three clichés in one paragraph! Clichés that have been regurgitated over and over by millions of uninformed American parrots. Foxman's act reminds me of a hilarious stand-up comedy routine performed by Jewish comedian Jerry Seinfeld. While making fun of an uncle of his who sees anti-Semites under every rock, Seinfeld recalls the time when his uncle was served cold soup in a restaurant. Upon realizing that his soup is cold, the uncle turns to Seinfeld and says: "You see that cook back there? He's an anti-Semite!"

Was Tim McVeigh the unwitting "patsy" who was used by an intelligence service? Don't discount the possibility of Mossad or CIA involvement in the Oklahoma City bombing. They had the motive (hatred of the anti-Zionist militias), the means (C-4 explosives), and the opportunity ("art students").

Of America's major networks, only Fox News made a meager attempt to investigate some of these mysteries, but Fox was quickly silenced by Zionist pressure. This alone is evidence of criminal activity! Before his excellent work was silenced, Fox's Carl Cameron reported this amazing bit of information:

> Investigators within the DEA, INS, and FBI have all told FOX News that to pursue or even suggest Israeli spying is considered career suicide.[26]

Did you catch that? If a Federal investigator dares to "even suggest" Israeli spying, he has committed "career suicide"! And if a journalist like Fox's Cameron dares to bring this scandal to light, he is told to shut his mouth. If they persist, they may even be called "anti-Semitic"—a label which has served as the "kiss of death" for many a career.

This means the Zionist Mafia can do whatever it wants, whenever it wants, and however it wants—including orchestrating, financing, executing and covering up the true story of events in the Middle East, the 9-11 massacre, and the ensuing "War on Terrorism."

Do you remember the Mossad's "warning" about the 200 "Al-Qaeda terrorists" said to have been preparing major attacks in the US?[27] At the time of this writing, we are two years into the largest investigation in American history, and not one of these "200 terrorists" has yet to be uncovered.[28] But 200 Israeli spies were uncovered, among them many military members, electronics experts, wiretapping and phone tapping specialists, and explosives experts with the skill to bring down tall buildings.[29] They were uncovered, and set free to terrorize us another day.

Logic and common sense led to the conclusion that the "200 Al-Qaeda terrorists" were in reality 200 Zionist terrorists sent to frame the Arabs for terrorist attacks and drag America into a war. For the first time since the British invasion of the War of 1812, the United States was invaded by what can truly be described as an invisible foreign army. The Israeli military invaders were aided and abetted by highly placed sympathizers in the media and government. And not 1 in 1000 Americans is even aware of these events!

In March 2003, a suspicious incident took place at New York's La Guardia Airport. CNN actually ran a quick caption about a woman whose bag was found by La Guardia screeners to contain a vial of anthrax. There was no follow up report afterwards. The airport terminal was evacuated, 10 people were treated because they felt sick, a screener was treated for a rash, and the powder initially tested positive for anthrax. Capital 9 News of Albany, New York reported on March 22:

> The central terminal of La Guardia Airport was evacuated.
> It happened Friday when a gas mask and white powder
> were found in an Israeli woman's bag. She was traveling
> from Israel to Texas. The first test came up positive for
> anthrax, but a second test proved negative.[30]

Reuters News Service confirmed that 10 people were sickened by the substance and treated:

> Authorities discovered a suspicious package containing an
> unknown powdery substance Friday at La Guardia Airport
> and partially evacuated the main terminal, police said.

A New York Fire Department spokesman said 10 people were apparently sickened by the unknown substance and were being treated at the scene.[31]

New York Newsday added that an Airport screener developed a rash soon after the incident:

> Wilkins said one screener reported a red rash on one of her hands after the incident, which he said may or may not be related to the powder. The screener was treated with alcohol and not taken to the hospital, Wilkins said.[32]

That's when the predictable FIB, I mean FBI coverup went into effect. A "second test" for anthrax proved negative, the woman's gas mask was just a "common Israeli safety precaution," the screener's rash was caused by her "latex gloves," the cause of the 10 airport illnesses was "unknown," and the Israeli woman and the story were never heard from again.

On December 11, 2002, Senator Bob Graham (D-FL), a leading member of the Senate Intelligence Committee, appeared as a guest on the *PBS Newshour* with Gwen Ifill. Graham surprised Ifill by expressing his belief that a foreign government or governments had to have funded and supported the hijackers. Here's part of the exchange:

> IFILL: Are you suggesting that you are convinced that there was a state sponsor behind 9/11?
>
> GRAHAM: I think there is very compelling evidence that at least some of the terrorists were assisted not just in financing—although that was part of it—by a sovereign foreign government and that we have been derelict in our duty to track that down, make the further case, or find the evidence that would indicate that that is not true and we can look for other reasons why the terrorists were able to function so effectively in the United States.
>
> IFILL: Do you think that will ever become public, which countries you're talking about?

Now listen to Graham's bombshell:

> GRAHAM: It will become public at some point when it's turned over to the archives, but that's 20 or 30 years from

now. And we need to have this information now because it's relevant to the threat that the people of the United States are facing today.[33]

Senator Graham is suggesting that US intelligence knows which foreign government helped the terrorists, but the government isn't going to tell us for another 30 years! Given the current state of anti-Muslim war hysteria being promoted by the media and government, common sense dictates that if an Arab government were ever discovered to have sponsored 9-11, we'd be seeing the evidence night and day on the controlled media, and hearing about it non-stop from all the President's warmongers as well as the Israeli-occupied US Congress and Senate. This alone is evidence that no Arab government was involved in 9-11.

It can't be an Arab government. Why would any Arab government sponsor "Al-Qaeda," an organization dedicated to overthrowing what it sees as corrupt, US-backed Arab governments? What Arab government would have incentive to attack America—its best oil purchasing customer? What Arab government would have the ability to shield itself from US media exposure? What Arab government would be so suicidal, so hell-bent on its own destruction, as to attack a mighty nuclear superpower like the United States? So who, if not an Arab government could be the chief sponsor of 9-11? Again, let's go back to Fox News quoting an FBI official. Pay close attention to the specific language used:

> Evidence linking these Israelis to 9-11 is classified. I cannot tell you about the evidence that has been gathered. It is classified information.[34]

In order for evidence "linking these Israelis to 9-11" to become classified, the evidence has to have existed in the first place! Furthermore, it must have been very, very serious stuff indeed. Only the really ugly stuff merits the distinction of being "classified!"

It may be possible that the good Senator doesn't know, himself, which country or countries are involved. Graham may still be under the delusion that it's an Arab government. Or, perhaps he's a disgusted patriot just trying to throw a subtle shot at Israel in his own way, without actually having to commit "career suicide" as have so many other anti-Zionist politicians in the past. History will reveal the truth one day, just as it did for Pearl Harbor. The trouble is, by that time, no one will care anymore about 9-11 and this phony "War on Terrorism." The American attention span does not reach to 20 or 30 years. It's closer to 20–30 minutes, about the length of an average Dan Rather, Peter Jennings or Tom Brokaw infomercial.

History always repeats itself. But who will teach this history to the American people when the Zionists control the information industry? The Zionist Mafia and their slathering careerist henchmen in media, government, academia, talk-radio, and business have all the bases covered.

17

Whistleblowers, Whistleblowers, Whistleblowers

The FBI Agents Who Tried To Prevent 9-11

The FBI's field agents are "the good guys." It's the spineless careerists at the top who have corrupted the agency. In the critical weeks and months leading up to that fateful day, numerous clues were picked up by loyal FBI field agents. Some of these agents were so alarmed at what they thought was an unfolding terror plot, they tried to convince their superiors to investigate deeper. These agents were either ignored, threatened, driven out of their positions, or fired.

Each of these FBI agents thought they were on the trail of an Arab terror plot, and unless they've read this book, they probably still believe so. We can forgive them their ignorance if they haven't realized yet that the trail they were on was not that of Arab terrorists, but rather Mossad agents impersonating Arab terrorists. The essential point is that these agents were on to something big that forces in high places clearly did not want them digging into.

Foremost among these agents was the FBI's Chief of Counter Terrorism, John O'Neill. In an article titled "John O'Neill was an FBI agent with an obsession: the growing threat of Al-Qaeda," the *New Yorker* magazine explains O'Neill's single-minded obsession with exposing what he believed were Al-Qaeda cells operating inside the US.[1] Time and time again the aggressive and outspoken Irishman expressed his frustration at having his hands tied by superiors. Eventually he quit the FBI (some say in protest) and accepted the position as Head of Security at, of all places, the World Trade Center. In a tragic twist of irony, O'Neill never got his chance to say, "See, I told you so." He was killed on September 11.

There is FBI Special Agent Robert Wright. The public interest law firm, Judicial Watch is representing agent Wright. Wright claims he was met with retaliation and threats from his bosses and from the Justice Department who told him they wanted his probes to go no further.[2] Wright maintains if his investigation had been allowed to continue, the attacks could have been prevented. He described for ABC News how he was held back by supervisors even after he presented them with evidence of criminal activity. Said Wright:

> The supervisor who was there from headquarters was right straight across from me and started yelling at me: "You will not open criminal investigations. I forbid any of you. You will not open criminal investigations against any of these intelligence subjects."[3]

There is FBI Special Agent, John Vincent, who corroborated Wright's story for ABC News.[4]

There is Chicago Federal Prosecutor, Mark Flessner who also wanted to pursue an investigation into what he believed was an Al-Qaeda terror cell. He too was blocked by his US Justice Department superiors. An angry Flessner claims:

> There were powers bigger than I was in the Justice Department and within the FBI that simply were not going to let the building of a criminal case happen. And it didn't happen.[5]

There is FBI agent Coleen Rowley. The gutsy Rowley wrote a 13-page letter to FBI Director, Robert Mueller in which she actually accuses the director of her own agency of "a subtle skewing of the facts."[6] Rowley's letter also charged that the agency refused to react to evidence of a pending terror plot. According to Rowley the FBI's obstruction was so blatant, she and some of her fellow agents jokingly speculated that key FBI personnel must have been moles working for Osama bin Laden![7]

Rowley's main point of contention was the agency's failure to go after Zacharias Moussoui, the "20th hijacker," even after his highly worried flight school instructor reported his suspicious behavior to the FBI. Moussoui, you will recall, was the French Algerian who couldn't speak French to his flight school instructor.

There is FBI agent Sibel Edmunds. Edmunds was an FBI wiretap translator. She claims that another FBI translator was working for the Mossad and that the Mossad also tried to recruit Edmunds to make phony translations for the purpose of misdirecting investigations. When agent Edmunds refused, the Mossad threatened her safety![8] When she brought these allegations to the attention of her superiors, she was fired for being "disruptive." The *Washington Post* briefly reported this story without mentioning the name of the nation that tried to recruit Edmunds. But the *Post* did reveal that Edmunds and the other translator "trace their ethnicity" to this certain "Middle Eastern" country.[9] Agent Sibel Edmunds is not an Arab. Edmunds is Jewish. Therefore, we know that the "Middle Eastern" nation which the *Post* chose not to name is Israel. (No big surprise there!)

Sibel Edmunds deserves a lot of credit for defying the Mossad and blowing the whistle to her superiors. Instead, she was fired for her patriotic efforts, proving once again that Zionists are willing to hurt innocent Jews.

There is FBI agent John M. Cole, program manager for FBI intelligence investigations covering India, Pakistan, and Afghanistan. In the same *Washington Post* story about Edmunds, it was reported that Cole also wrote a letter to FBI chief Mueller warning him about lax security procedures in the hiring of translators.[10]

Dedicated agents such as O'Neill, Wright, Vincent, Flessner, Rowley, Cole, Edmunds and many others who have spoken anonymously, had to be stopped from going after "Muslim terrorists." If not so obstructed, they would in time come to discover they weren't really Al-Qaeda terrorists, but rather Mossad agents posing as Muslims!! Not only were investigations blocked before 9-11; they continue to be blocked after 9-11. The coverup is so blatant, members of both the

House and Senate Intelligence committees complained directly to CIA Director George Tenet and Attorney General John Ashcroft. The *Los Angeles Times* reported:

> Lawmakers leading the investigation of intelligence failures surrounding the 9-11 attacks are increasingly concerned that the CIA and Justice department are actively impeding their efforts ... The flare up centers on obstacles congressional investigators say the agencies have strewn in their path."[11]

That's exactly what FBI agents O'Neil, Wright, Rowley, Edmunds, and Cole said happened to them when they tried to investigate before the attacks! As for CIA Director George Tenet, his "incompetence" as CIA chief is such that Senators Thompson (TN) and Shelby (AL) have been trying to force his resignation.[12]

The 9-11 attacks represent the biggest intelligence "failure" since the Bay of Pigs fiasco in 1961, and yet, Bush won't touch George Tenet. Perhaps he's mindful of what happened to the last US President who dared to confront a protected CIA Director. (John F. Kennedy fired CIA chief Allen Dulles in 1961 because of the Bay of Pigs disaster. Dulles later served on the Warren Commission, which covered up many of the facts surrounding Kennedy's assassination.)

The government/media complex insists these botched investigations were the result of innocent mistakes caused by "bureaucratic incompetence" or "lack of inter-departmental communication."

How is it that the CIA and FBI could not infiltrate these "Al-Qaeda cells," but a 21 year old kid from California named John Walker Lindh was able to merely convert to Islam, show up in Afghanistan and supposedly attend one of Bin Laden's "terror camps"? If "incompetence" is to blame, then where are all of the reprimands that should have been issued against the "negligent" officials who ignored the warnings? To date, we have yet to hear of a single FBI, DOJ, CIA or INS employee who has been fired, demoted or even just verbally reprimanded over the mishandling of these terror leads. Where are all of the sacrificial scapegoats that governments are famous for throwing overboard in order to "cover their asses"?

Why are clowns like Mueller and Tenet still allowed to keep their jobs? Why isn't the media attempting to specifically identify who these "incompetent" bureaucrats really are? What higher powers are protecting these "incompetents" and why? There should be "hell to pay" for 9-11, but it seems that the only ones getting fired or reprimanded are the aforementioned agents who actually tried to stop 9-11!

It's bad enough that these "incompetent bureaucrats" have gone unpunished for their deadly "negligence." But the outrage goes much deeper than that. In December of 2002, Marion Bowman, the FBI official who killed Colleen Rowley's Moussoui investigation, actually received a meritorious service award and a big fat cash bonus from FBI Director Robert Mueller!

Senator Charles Grassley of Iowa was so shocked to hear of this award, he is demanding answers from FBI chief Mueller. The *Washington Times* reported:

> FBI Director Robert S. Mueller III has been asked by a senior member of the Senate Judiciary Committee to justify an award he gave to an FBI official who refused requests by Minneapolis agents for a warrant to search the computer of terror suspect Zacharias Moussoui.
>
> Sen. Charles E. Grassley, (R-IA), described as "shocking" Mr. Mueller's decision to give the Presidential Rank of Meritorious Service award to Marion "Spike" Bowman, head of the FBI's national security law unit.
>
> "By granting this award and a monetary bonus, you are sending the wrong signal to those agents who fought—sometimes against senior FBI bureaucrats at headquarters—to prevent the [September 11] attacks."
>
> Agent Coleen Rowley, said the agents faced a "roadblock" when they sought the Moussaoui search warrant, and they became so frustrated at the lack of response that they

sought to bypass the chain of command and notify the CIA directly—but were reprimanded.

The awards included cash bonuses of between 20 percent or 35 percent of each recipient's base salary.[13]

It must be nice to have a job where such a colossal screw-up— a screw-up that led to the preventable murders of 3000 people—is rewarded with meritorious service awards and bonus money! Who says crime doesn't pay?

Systematic and repeated consistency of "errors" is a sign of treason, not incompetence. Bowman, Mueller, Tenet and so many others know what they are doing. Like the 1919 Chicago White Sox—whose crooked baseball players "threw" the World Series after they were bribed by a gambler—the likes of Tenet and Mueller have been "throwing the game." And just like the 1919 White Sox, they'll occasionally do or say something right from time to time just to "make it look good."

(Interesting bit of trivia ... the gambler who fixed the 1919 World Series was a Zionist gangster named Arnold Rothstein.)

Did I mention that all FBI criminal investigations fall under the jurisdiction of yet another Zionist named Michael Chertoff? Chertoff is the Director of the Criminal Division of the US Justice Department. FBI chief Mueller has to answer to Chertoff on criminal matters. We have Chertoff to thank for those 200 Israeli "movers" and "art students" being set free. Chertoff is also the man responsible for putting the outspoken Congressman James Trafficant in jail. Trafficant was hated by the pro-Israel lobby for his tough positions against Israel.

18

Foxman's Famous Flunkies

Working hand in hand with the Zionist-run media, the Zionist-run Pentagon and Zionist Congressional Lobby (AIPAC) is the Mossad affiliated Anti-Defamation League (ADL). Although professing to be a civil rights organization interested only in protecting individual freedom and fighting bigotry, the ADL is in reality a political attack group that specializes in destroying the careers and reputations of anyone (Jews and non-Jews alike) who criticizes Zionism or Israel.

The list of prominent politicians, writers, artists and intellectuals that have been viciously attacked by the ADL and other Zionist affiliates is as long as it is diverse. It includes conservatives such as Pat Buchanan and Joe Sobran, liberals such as Marlon Brando and Gore Vidal, Republicans such as Senator Charles Percy and Congressman Paul Findley, Democrats such as Senators William Fulbright and Congressman James Trafficant, black political figures such as Congresswoman Cynthia McKinney and poet Amiri Baraka, and even fellow Jews such as Noam Chomsky and recently deceased Senator Paul Wellstone.

Although he himself was Jewish and very pro-Israel, Senator Paul Wellstone [D-MN], was strongly opposed to war with Iraq and he was also an outspoken supporter of Palestinian rights. He had also met with Yasser Arafat and publicly supported the creation of a Palestinian state. Wellstone and his wife were killed in a mysterious plane crash just days before his imminent re-election. It would be very hard to prove that Wellstone was assassinated, but the fact that AIPAC, Bush, and Cheney were so obsessed with getting him out of the US Senate is something to think about. There's nothing that irritates the Zionists more than a "self-hating Jew."

Adding to the intrigue is the fact that Wellstone's Senate seat was then won by Norm Coleman, a hard-core Zionist Republican who was hand-picked by Bush-Cheney and backed strongly by AIPAC. Just days after his inauguration, Freshman Coleman was leap-frogged over dozens of senior GOP Senators and awarded the prestigious Chairmanship on the powerful Senate Investigations committee.

When not preoccupied with destroying the careers and reputations of "anti-Semites" and "self-hating Jews," the ADL keeps itself occupied with other such controversial efforts as:

- Pressuring small towns across America to remove religious Christmas displays.
- Pressuring school boards to remove "anti-Semitic" books, such as William Shakespeare's *Merchant of Venice*, from the curriculum.
- Pressuring schools and public libraries to install Internet filters designed to block access to "anti-Semitic" websites.
- Pressuring state governments to impose mandatory Holocaust education (indoctrination) programs for all elementary and High Schools. (Sixteen states now have such laws!)
- Pressuring US Presidents to pardon Zionist criminals and traitors like the fugitive financier, Mark Rich and the notorious atomic spy, Jonathan Pollard.

The ADL's current Director, Abe Foxman has declared, "Anti-Zionism is Anti-Semitism. Period."[1]

In a furious response to growing worldwide speculation of Zionist involvement in 9-11 (a commonly held opinion in both Europe and the Muslim world), dishonest Abe added:

When we first heard of the charge that Jews, Israel and the Mossad were responsible for the Sept. 11 attacks, most of us chuckled. But it didn't take long to realize that it was not a joking matter, that it wasn't anything to laugh about.

Today you can travel the Arab world, Asia, and Europe, and read in newspapers and hear on radio and TV the big hideous lie that has become a truth—that Jews bring about a situation in their interest in order to put the blame on somebody else. How classically anti-Semitic! [2]

Methinks Foxman doth protest too much!

When someone like Abe Foxman starts raving and ranting "anti-Semitism ... anti-Semitism," it's usually a good indication that some brave soul has struck a nerve by daring to tell the truth about the Zionist Mafia. The ADL not only defines "anti-Semitism," but also tells writers and politicians what to think and who to blame for "terrorist attacks." The list of political luminaries that Foxman carries around in his hip pocket like so many spare coins is truly impressive.

This explains FBI Director Mueller's highly pathetic, and revealing speech before the ADL's 24th Annual National Leadership Conference held in May of 2002:

> I have long admired and respected the work of ADL, and I appreciate your longstanding support of the FBI. I know that under my predecessor, Louis Freeh, this partnership reached new heights ... I am absolutely committed to building on that relationship. We in the FBI tremendously value your perspectives and your partnership. Your insights and research into extremism are particularly helpful to us, shedding light on the changing nature of the terrorist threats facing America. Your support of hate crime and terrorist investigations, which are now front and center in the work of the FBI, is essential to us. And the training and education you provide for the FBI and for law enforcement have never been more relevant. That includes the conference on extremist and terrorist threats you are sponsoring this month at the FBI Academy.[3]

The FBI is in "partnership" with the Zionist ADL and relies upon this smear group for "insights, research, education and training!" Over at the CIA, the situation is even worse. Just listen to the "incompetent" CIA Director, George Tenet as he expresses his love for ADL Director Abe Foxman at a dinner in Foxman's honor:

> I searched for a Greek word that best captures the way I feel, and it suddenly came to me ... The word, from ancient Greek, is "rabbi." ... "Rabbi" means 'my teacher,' not just 'teacher,' but 'my teacher.' And Abe, that is what you have been to me and to so many others in this room. You have ... educated me about anti-Semitism and made me understand it far better than I ever did before, and like the greatest of rabbis, you just don't teach the ethical precepts of the Torah, you live them.[4]

Tenet's predecessor at the CIA, James Woolsey, is no better. Woolsey now serves on the Zionist controlled Defense Policy Board under Richard Perle and has been in the forefront of the fraudulent effort to link Iraq to 9-11.

Here are more declarations of love and affection for the known criminal, slanderer, liar, and Israeli agent Foxman, issued by some of the most powerful men in America. At that same dinner, then president Bill—"I'd-fight-and-die-for-Israel"—Clinton said:

> Abe, throughout your life you've been a guiding light—to the people of our nation, to the citizens of Israel, and to those fighting for peace and justice around the world.[5]

Saint Rudy the Recycler added: "I thank Abe for the people of the City of New York, and personally, for all that he's done ..."[6]

Future president, then Texas governor, George Bush also paid his tribute to Foxman: "Throughout the years, you have prodded the conscience of the world."[7]

At a 2001 ADL conference, pro-Israel Attorney general, (and Evangelical religious fanatic) John Ashcroft thanked the notoriously anti-Christian ADL: "I want to express personally my gratitude to the ADL for its assistance that it provides to us."[8]

Study some of the above comments closely. "Partner" … "My rabbi" … "Guiding Light to our nation" … "Prodder of the Conscience of the World."

Is this the language of sincere admiration? Or does it sound more like the type of exaggerated flattery that awestruck subordinates might use to please and pacify a demanding boss? Think about it. Didn't anyone ever tell these important public officials of ours that when the FBI raided the California offices of the ADL in 1993, they found that the ADL had computerized files on nearly 10,000 people across the country, and that more than 75 percent of the information had been illegally obtained from police, FBI files and state drivers license data banks?[9] Are they not aware that the San Francisco Superior Court awarded $150,000 in court judgments against the Anti-Defamation League in connection with this FBI bust?[10] Are they not aware that the ADL has lobbied on behalf of Federal criminals like fugitive Mark Rich and atomic spy and traitor Jonathan Pollard?

What other group in America could get away with not only stealing FBI files (a Federal offense!) but then becoming "partners" with the FBI? What purpose would the ADL have for these files? Why would men like FBI Director Mueller, Attorney General Ashcroft, CIA Director Tenet, and Presidents Clinton and Bush disregard the fact that the ADL is a criminal group that was caught spying on US citizens by their own FBI? Why does Mueller ignore the insights of his own agents while thanking the criminal and slanderous ADL for its "advice"?

Mueller, Tenet, Ashcroft, Bush, Clinton, Giuliani, etc. are empty, careerist "yes men" who understand that it doesn't pay to defy the Zionist Mafia, lest Foxman and his Mossad buddies reveal some juicy little secret to the Zionist media, a secret contained in those stolen FBI files. For as long as they remain useful, these obedient careerist whores are promoted, honored and hyped by the Zionist-controlled media, leaving behind honest field agents like Wright, Rowley, Edmunds and Cole!

In case you're wondering where Abe Foxman stood on the issue of going to war with Iraq, understand that Foxman denounced anti-war demonstrations in Europe and the United States as having "anti-Semitic" overtones. Foxman made his desire for war very clear in an op-ed piece titled "Blame the Terrorists, Not Israel." Here is his recommendation (marching orders) to America's leaders (his ass-kissers):

> The American willingness to protect other states in the region from extremists, whether Saddam Hussein or Osama Bin Laden, makes America the prime enemy ... Words and international resolutions are meaningless in the face of such a threat. Preemptive action is the only real deterrent ...

We will take the war to them. Of course, there will be those here and abroad who will try to divert our government and people from its necessary mission. One way is the suggestion that this happened because US support of Israel breeds hatred of us in the Arab world. If only America had backed off from Israel, it is said none of this would have happened.

Fortunately, those distortions are scarcely heard, but inevitably as time goes on, more voices to this effect will surface. It should be so obvious how patently absurd such charges are ... Israel is relevant to this threat, but only in the sense that Israel stands for the same values as America, that Israel will be a loyal ally—strategically, militarily, and emotionally—in this long-term struggle for the very future of the world.[11]

And when Dishonest Abe talks, you'd better believe that America's leaders listen!

19

The Anthrax Letters: Yet Another Anti-Arab Frame-Up Attempt

On October 3, 2001, an Egyptian-American scientist named Dr. Ayaad Assaad sat terrified in a vault-like interrogation room at an FBI office in Washington DC. It was not yet known that a pair of letters containing deadly anthrax had been mailed to NBC Newsman Tom Brokaw and US Senator Tom Daschle. Five people would die as a result of the anthrax mailings which had been posted from New Jersey. Billions of pieces of mail were delayed, causing the US Post Office to suffer huge losses.

The news media ran nothing but anthrax stories night and day. Politicians and commentators speculated that Osama Bin Laden or Saddam Hussein were behind the deadly letters. Why was the FBI questioning Assaad?

Just before the anthrax murders were committed, someone had sent the FBI an anonymous letter accusing Dr. Assaad of being a bio-terrorist with a grudge against the United States.[1] The letter was sent on September 25—before the first anthrax case was even diagnosed. The FBI agents soon were convinced that the anonymous letter was a hoax and a frame-up attempt. Assaad was cleared of suspicion and released. Assaad later told the *Hartford Courant* of Connecticut:

> I was so angry when I read the letter, I broke out in tears. Whoever this person is knew in advance what was going to

happen and created a suitable, well-fitted scapegoat for this action. You do not need to be a Nobel Laureate to put two and two together.[2]

If we find out who would have wanted to frame Dr. Assad in particular, and Arabs in general, we will likely find out who was behind the anthrax murders. That the wording of the anthrax letters was contrived in such a manner as to frame Arabs/Muslims is so self-evident, even a mentally retarded child could see through it. Here is the wording of the Daschle letter:

> You cannot stop us. We have this anthrax. You die now. Are you afraid? Death to America. Death to Israel. Allah is great.[3]

And the Brokaw letter:

> This is next. Take Penicillin now. Death to America. Death to Israel. Allah is great.[4]

Give me a break!!!!!!!!!! Ask yourself: who would want to frame Arabs? Who would want to link the interests of the US and the interests of Israel in such an obvious way? Remember the Lavon Affair? Remember the USS Liberty? Remember the dancing Israelis? Remember Netanyahu saying 9-11 was good for US-Israeli relations?

A good place to start searching for the culprit is the US bio-weapons lab at Fort Detrick, Maryland. The Ames strain of anthrax has in fact been traced to Fort Detrick, where Assaad once worked until he was laid off in 1997. After he was let go from Fort Detrick, Assaad filed a federal discrimination suit based upon the brutal abuse and harassment that he had endured from some highly suspicious co-workers.

In 1991, Assaad found an 8-page poem in his mailbox which became a courtroom exhibit. The poem had 235 lines, many of them lewd and sexually explicit, mocking Assaad. Along with the poem, the perpetrators left Assaad a rubber camel with a large penis attached to it.[5]

This was an obvious attempt to mock Assaad's Arab ethnicity. Assaad said that when he brought the poem to the attention of his supervisor, Col. David Franz, Franz kicked him out of his office![6]

These were not immature college kids. This outrageous emotional abuse was carried out by highly trained scientists who obviously wanted to get rid of Assaad.

The scientist who was the ring-leader in these horrible attacks on Dr. Assaad was Dr. Lt. Col. Philip Zack. Philip Zack was to "voluntarily" leave Fort Detrick shortly after Assaad brought Zack's poem and camel to the attention of his supervisors.[7] Strike one on Dr. Zack!

In an unrelated matter, another Fort Detrick researcher, Dr. Mary Beth Downs told army investigators that on several occasions in January and February of 1992, she had come to work to discover that someone had been conducting anthrax research after hours.[8]

Who could that have been? Documents from that 1992 inquiry confirm that an unauthorized person was observed on a surveillance camera being admitted into the lab at 8:40 PM on January 23, 1992. Who was this unauthorized person caught sneaking into the bio-weapons lab, during the same time period that anthrax research was being done after hours? It turned out to be Lt. Col. Philip Zack![9] The same Zack who was forced to resign a year earlier because of his horrible abuse of Dr. Assaad. Strike two on Dr. Zack!

Why would Dr. Zack and others have such an animosity toward Dr. Assaad? What would motivate him to help write a 235-line hate poem? What motive would he have to frame Arabs for the deadly anthrax murders?

Research into the name "Zack" reveals it is a fairly common Jewish surname, derived from the Old Testament "Zacharias." Dr. Zack is Jewish, and given his obvious, fanatical hatred of Arabs, we can safely deduce that he is a hard core Zionist. Strike three on Dr. Zack!

All of the above is public information. Assaad's 1990's legal proceedings, Dr. Down's testimony, the surveillance video of Zack sneaking into Fort Detrick one year after he had "resigned"—it's all there. The *Hartford Courant* exposed all of these facts[10] as did the *Toronto Globe and Mail*,[11] the *Seattle Times*,[12] and other publications. Just the facts contained in the *Hartford Courant* story alone should be enough to at least indict Philip Zack. So why didn't we see Dr. Zack's face on our TV screens? Why hasn't

Dr. Zack been given a lie detector test? What forces in the media and the government are protecting Dr. Zack from being exposed as the logical prime suspect?

The plot thickens (and sickens) even more. It is not my intent to smear, defame, or offend Jewish people. But to not mention the ethnicity of certain players in this fantastic drama would be like writing an exposé on the Italian Mafia without mentioning that its major players are Italians. Remember, some of the Zionists' harshest critics are themselves Jewish.

Dr. Assaad had been cleared and Dr. Zack was coming under a small amount of media and FBI suspicion. Enter, from stage left, one Barbara Rosenberg, a Jewish environmentalist, professor and political activist with no expertise in bio-warfare.[13] Rosenberg suddenly went public with the claim that she knew who the anthrax killer was.[14] She was supported in this effort by another Zionist *New York Times* journalist named Nicholas D. Kristof, who openly called for the arrest of the innocent American scientist named Dr. Stephen Hatfill.[15]

Quietly and behind the scenes, Rosenberg began directing investigators toward Dr. Hatfill (and therefore away from Dr. Zack). The *Washington Post* confirmed that it was Rosenberg who helped put authorities on the trail of the innocent Dr. Hatfill.[16]

The name of Hatfill trickled forth from the news media. In a matter of weeks, the trickle became a media flood. Dr. Hatfill got the "Richard Jewell" treatment from the media and Hatfill became a household name. (Richard Jewell was the security guard who was falsely accused by the FBI and mass media of staging the Atlanta Olympics bombing in 1996. Jewell later sued NBC and settled his case out of court.)

Hatfill called a news conference to protest his innocence. There was never even a shred of evidence against him and he even passed an FBI lie detector test.[17] But the Zionist-controlled media lynch mob, led by the evil Rosenberg and the yellow journalist Kristof, continued to pursue and harass Hatfill. Dr. Hatfill will never be imprisoned, but his life and career have been destroyed by these false allegations and the media hype. Lt. Col. Zack is off the hook.

What these mad Zionist scientists and their media brethren have done to Dr. Assaad and Dr. Hatfill is monstrous beyond belief. It is clear that these anthrax letters were first intended to be an anti-Arab frame-up with Assaad meant to take the blame. When that didn't work, these fanatical Zionists (who always stick together like glue!) put the media and the FBI on poor Dr. Hatfill's back, and wrecked his career and reputation in the process.

Why hasn't Dr. Zack been given an FBI lie detector test???? Ask FBI boss and ADL "partner" Robert Mueller!

20

The Cult of Christian Zionism

As we have seen, many non-Jews aid and abet the Zionist Mafia for various reasons ranging from fear, to ambition—to just plain gullibility. The worst elements in the gullible category would have to be the mentally deranged Evangelical Christian Fundamentalists (funny-mentalists) who blindly and unconditionally support Israel's terror campaign because of some obscure passage in the Old Testament.

The funny-mentalist cult believes that God wants the Jews to have Palestine and "He will bless us if we bless Israel." Millions of Falwell's fools and Robertson's robots actually believe that by blindly supporting the murderous state of Israel, Jesus Christ will return and zap them up into Heaven! One has to wonder if the Mossad doesn't have some juicy little sex secret (a la Jimmy Swaggert/ Jim Baker) on these multi-millionaire hypocrite preachers.

And oh how the Christian-hating Zionists are playing these brainwashed Evangelical fools! Terrorist Menachem Begin even gave Jerry Falwell a lear jet in 1979![1] That's right! The same bloody murderer that John F. Kennedy, Hannah Arendt and Albert Einstein refused to meet with, the same terrorist who was the mastermind behind the King David Hotel bombing, the same butcher who was in charge of the massacre of Christians at Deir Yassin [see Chapter 5] gave Reverend Falwell a lear jet! Israel later awarded Falwell the Vladimir Jabotinsky award during a fancy dinner ceremony in 1981.

In July of 2002, the Zionist Organization of America (ZOA) awarded Pat Robertson the State of Israel Friendship Award at its annual "Salute to Israel" Dinner. Robertson has also been recognized with the Millennium Jerusalem 2000 Council Award by the State of Israel Jerusalem Heritage Study Programs, Defender of Israel Award in 1994 by the Christians' Israel Public Action Campaign, and the Distinguished Merit of Citation Award in 1979 by the National Conference of Christians and Jews.[2]

Robertson once claimed that God himself timed the sudden exposure of the Monica Lewinsky scandal to protect Israel from the growing pressure Bill Clinton was placing on Israel at that exact point in time. [CBN, 700 Club].[3]

Actually, Robertson was partially right about the coincidental timing of the two events. Only it wasn't God who arranged for Monica Lewinsky to be secretly tape recorded, it was the Zionist Lucianne Goldberg. [See Chapter 8.] Robertson knows this. The son of a former US Senator, Robertson is an intelligent man who understands all too well how these Machiavellian political chess games are played behind the scenes.

Apparently these funny-mentalists have never taken the time to actually read the NEW Testament, where Jesus Christ talks about peace, love, mercy, and the brotherhood of man. Before the Zionist financiers of his day conspired to have him crucified, Jesus had attacked them with a whip! I am convinced that if The Prince of Peace ever did return to earth, he would do likewise to Messrs. Sharon, Falwell, and Robertson!

The funny-mentalist Evangelicals might also benefit from reading the Koran; Islam's Holy Book. They would no doubt be surprised (as I was) to learn that:

- Muslims regard Jesus as a Holy Prophet born to the Virgin Mary (unlike the Rabbinic Talmud which vilifies Jesus).
- The Koran describes Christians and Hebrews as also being "people of God" whose communities are to be protected and respected under Islamic law (as indeed they had been throughout the Ottoman Empire for many centuries).

• Misunderstood terms such as "jihad" and "slay the infidels" appear in the context of self-defense against the brutal persecution that early Muslims had to endure at the hands of the pagan Kings of Arabia.

Christian Zionists fail to recognize these facts. The irony of the Christian Zionist love affair with the Zionists is that Christian doctrine is actually far closer to what the Muslims believe than it is to Judaism. Yasser Arafat's wife is actually a Christian as are Iraq's Minister Tariq Aziz and thousands of other Palestinian Arabs. Deep down, the Zionists hate the Evangelicals almost as much as they do the Muslims. It is the Zionists who run Hollywood, who churn out the blatantly anti-Christian junk that the Evangelicals are always complaining about! Next to "anti-Semitism," the smear terms "radical religious right" or "Christian right" are Abe Foxman's favorite slogans.

But rather than use God's greatest gift, our ability to think and reason, the funny-mentalists are content to let sanctimonious, Zionist-lovers like Jerry Falwell, Gary Bauer, Ralph Reed and Pat Robertson do their thinking for them. These "Christian-Zionist" multi-millionaires, who are highly influential within the GOP, have told their gullible audiences that the Islamic prophet Mohammed was a terrorist and a child abuser, while remaining silent as thousands of Palestinian Christians are humiliated and chased off their land by Sharon's killers. While the Israelis laid siege to the Church of the Nativity in Bethlehem, the funny-mentalists were raising funds to finance the oppressors of the Arab Christians of Palestine.

21

Follow the Phony Trail

Deductive Logic Reveals the True Culprits

Logical Conclusion Number One: 9-11 was carried out by either one of two groups:

GROUP 1: MUSLIM TERRORISTS seeking to avenge US policies in the Middle East, or

GROUP 2: ZIONIST TERRORISTS seeking to frame their enemies as a pretext for involving the US in a war against Arab/Muslim states.

THERE ARE NO OTHER LOGICAL SUSPECTS OTHER THAN THESE TWO, which leads us to . . .

Logical Conclusion Number Two: The true culprits wish to remain unknown.

We know this because Bin Laden strongly denied any involvement in 9-11 and suggested that the Zionists were behind it.[1] It is widely believed throughout the Arab and Muslim world (and even much of Europe) that Israeli and US elements staged 9-11 as a pretext for a war against the Islamic world. The Zionists and the US scoff at this idea and insist that Muslim terrorists carried out 9-11.

IN SHORT, GROUP 1 CLAIMS GROUP 2 DID IT, AND GROUP 2 CLAIMS GROUP 1 DID IT, which leads us to ...

Logical Conclusion Number Three: To escape punishment from an outraged United States, the true culprits would need to plant a false trail of "evidence" away from themselves and toward the other group.

Given that both Group 1 or Group 2 would be in serious trouble if it were discovered to be responsible for 9-11, and given the fact that each group blames the other, we would therefore expect the true culprit to attempt to divert the investigation toward the innocent group and away from itself. This trick is as old as crime itself. As surely as night follows day, a phony evidence trail would have had to surface following the 9-11 operation, WHICH LEADS US TO ...

Logical Conclusion Number Four: If we find what appears to be a false evidence trail, we will have found the true culprit.

By simply reversing the direction toward which the phony trail points, we can logically deduce who the true culprits were. Whichever group has phony-looking evidence directed toward it must therefore be the innocent group. Find the phony trail and you will find the guilty party, WHICH LEADS US TO ...

Logical Conclusion Number Five: The only trail that appears to be of suspicious origin points toward Muslims. Consider these very strange pieces of "evidence" that surfaced in the days following 9-11:

1. A few weeks before 9-11, Israeli Mossad officials flew to the US and met with leaders of the FBI and CIA. The Mossad claimed that a major terrorist attack was imminent and that the culprits would be Osama bin Laden and Iraq's Saddam Hussein. They gave no other details.[2]

2. After the attacks, there were widely publicized reports that the government had a tape recording of Bin Laden calling his mother just a few days before the attacks and telling her: "Something big is about to happen and you won't be hearing from me for awhile." This claim was broadcast repeatedly on every news network and convinced many people that Bin Laden was indeed guilty.

Weeks later, CNN corrected itself and revealed that the story turned out to be baseless. Although the story is now universally repudiated by even mainstream media, far fewer people ever heard the repudiation than the large number that heard the original hyped-up claim.[3]

3. Hours after the attacks, investigators received a report of a suspicious car left behind at Boston's Logan Airport by a group of belligerent Arabs. Inside the car, investigators find an Arab language flight manual and a Koran.[4] HOW CONVENIENT!

4. Again at Logan Airport, investigators "discovered" a suitcase belonging to "ringleader" Mohammed Atta—a suitcase that somehow didn't make it aboard the flight. (Why would someone pack a suitcase for a suicide mission?) Inside the suitcase they found another Koran, a fuel consumption calculator, a "suicide note," and a video tape of a Boeing 757.[5] HOW CONVENIENT!

5. At the fiery crash site in Pennsylvania, investigators "recovered" an identical copy of the Atta "suicide note."[6] The destruction at the crash site was so complete that the largest piece of human remains found was an 8-inch piece of spine.[7] Yet the letter survived the awesome crash and incineration unscathed. HOW CONVENIENT!

6. Days after the attacks, a slightly burned passport belonging to one of the "Saudi hijackers" was miraculously found just a few blocks away from the rubble of the World Trade Center.[8] HOW CONVENIENT!

7. On the eve of 9-11, supposed hijacker Ziad Jarrah mailed a self-incriminating farewell letter to his German girlfriend. "Luckily" for US investigators, the letter was "made out to the wrong address" and returned to the United States, where it found its way to the FBI. The BBC reported on the story as it appeared in the national German magazine, *Der Spiegel*:

> One of the 11 September hijackers sent his German girlfriend a farewell letter on the eve of the attacks, the German news magazine *Der Spiegel* has reported.

"I have done what I had to do," says the letter from Ziad Jarrah, urging his girlfriend to be proud of him, the magazine reported in its Monday edition.

But Jarrah apparently made a mistake when he wrote the German address, and the package was returned to the US, where it was passed to the FBI, said *Der Spiegel*.[9]

8. FBI Director Mueller even admitted that identity thefts were used in connection with 9-11.[10] As many as 7 of the 19 "Arab hijackers" are alive and well and some had reported their passports stolen in 1999.[11]

9. Weeks after 9-11, anthrax letters killed 5 people. The wording of the letters was designed to implicate Muslims. "Death to America. Death to Israel. Allah is great." It has long since been established that the anthrax came from a US army lab and was not mailed by Muslims.[12]

10. The Zionist-run Pentagon claimed to have found a "confession video" from Osama bin Laden. How convenient that the man who was clever enough to pull off 9-11 would suddenly become so careless and leave a self-incriminating video lying around Afghanistan. Independent translations of the barely audible video later exposed the US translation as "manipulative and inaccurate."[13] Other analyses of the video raises even more questions of fraud and doctoring.

11. It is then revealed that investigators also found a business card belonging to one of the hijackers at the Pennsylvania crash site. On the back of this miraculous business card is a telephone number linking one of the hijackers to the "20th hijacker," Zacharias Moussoui.[14] HOW CONVENIENT!

12. Also at the Pennsylvania crash site, another miracle passport belonging to "hijacker pilot" Ziad Jarrah was "found."[15] HOW CONVENIENT! Why were these hijackers carrying passports for internal domestic flights anyway?

13. The Friday before the attacks, three loud-mouthed drunken "hijackers" (Mohammed Atta and the Al-Shehhi brothers) made a memorable scene at a restaurant in Hollywood, Florida. (Keep the

name Hollywood, Florida in your mind for a moment.) The *London Telegraph* (and many other sources) tell us:

> Mohammed Atta, 33, who almost certainly was the Florida-trained pilot who rammed American Airlines Flight 11 into the north tower of the World Trade Centre, his cousin Marwan al-Shehhi, 23, and an Arab believed to be a brother of al-Shehhi, appeared to have been in a bibulous celebratory mood last week.

Tony Amos, the manager of Shuckums Oyster Bar and Restaurant in Hollywood (Florida) just north of Miami, was interviewed by the FBI and he and his barman and a waitress all identified Atta and his cousin as some hard drinkers who propped up the bar last Friday.

Atta's bill for three hours of vodka drinking came to $48 (£33). When he drunkenly disputed the charge, Mr Amos intervened. "Of course I can pay the bill," Atta told him. "I'm an airline pilot."[16]

Devout fundamentalist Muslim "martyrs" drinking vodka for three hours? And notice how Mohammed Atta purposely goes out of his way to tell the manager he was "an airline pilot." This is very similar to the way in which he purposely told his flight school instructor he was "leaving for Boston." [See Chapter 11.]

14. The night before the attacks, three loud-mouthed "hijackers" (one of them again being the "ringleader" Mohammed Atta) visited a Florida strip club where they again caused a scene and made a deliberate point of telling people about a pending terror attack. They then conveniently "forgot" yet another Koran at the bar! That makes THREE Korans that Mohammed and his boys left lying around for investigators to "discover" on 9-10 and 9-11! CBS News reported on September 14, 2001:

> The three men spewed anti-American sentiments in a bar and talked of impending bloodshed the night before the

terrorist attacks on New York and Washington, a Daytona Beach strip club manager interviewed by the FBI said Thursday.

They were talking about what a bad place America is. They said "Wait 'til tomorrow. America is going to see bloodshed," said John Kap, manager of the Pink Pony and Red Eyed Jack's Sports Bar. Kap said they made the claims to a bartender and a patron ... Kap said he told FBI investigators the men in his bar spent $200 to $300 apiece on lap dances and drinks, paying with credit cards. Kap said he gave the FBI credit card receipts, photocopied driver's licenses, a business card left by one man and a copy of the Quran—the sacred book of Islam—that was left at the bar.[17]

This one takes the grand prize! Devout, fundamentalist Muslim "martyrs" not only getting drunk, but fondling naked dancers just hours before they were scheduled to meet with God! These highly skilled secret operatives then jeopardized their mission by drawing attention to themselves while publicly bashing America and boasting about pending bloodshed, to take place the following day? And what on earth were they doing in Florida instead of Boston on the eve of 9-11 anyway? Didn't they realize that if either of their two early morning connecting flights (first to Maine, and then to Boston) were a bit delayed the next morning, their whole operation would have been at risk? And finally, they oh-so-conveniently forgot their business cards and Koran at the bar!

Who would take the Holy Book of Islam into a strip club? For what purpose? Were these "Muslims" reciting their prayers in between shots of vodka and "lap dances"? Just picture "Mohammed Atta" reading sacred scripture, holding his Koran open with one hand, while stuffing $5 bills inside a stripper's crotch string with the other! What a scene!

This Mohammed Atta character sure is an absent-minded fellow, isn't he? He "loses" his passport in 1999, he "forgets" how to speak German when his flight school instructor tries to make small talk with him [see Chapter 11], he "forgets" his suitcase before the

9-11 attacks (or perhaps he remembered at the last moment that he wasn't going to need a suitcase for a suicide mission!), he "forgets" a Koran in a Florida strip club, and then "forgets" yet two other Korans in Boston, and also "forgets" his Arabic language flight manual and "forgets" his fuel consumption calculator! How did this guy ever get to be an engineer?

My dear reader—no disrespect intended—but if you can't see through these little stunts as the obvious work of a team of "false flag" imposters, then you are either truly stupid and beyond all hope of rehabilitation, or you are just willfully blinded by your own cowardice.

So who, if not Mohammed Atta and his friends, could these drunken, womanizing, Koran-toting, "Muslims" of Florida actually have been? An excellent May 7, 2002 story written by Christopher Ketcham of *Salon* Magazine provides a clue. Ketcham writes about the Israeli "art student" spy ring that was uncovered in 2001. In an article entitled "The Israeli Art Student Mystery," Ketcham informs us:

> For almost two years, hundreds of young Israelis falsely claiming to be art students haunted federal offices ... No one knows why—and no one seems to want to find out.

> In HOLLYWOOD, (Florida) several students lived at 4220 Sheridan St., just down the block from the 3389 Sheridan St. apartment where terrorist mastermind Mohammed Atta holed up with three other Sept. 11 plotters. Many of the students, the DEA report noted, had backgrounds in Israeli military intelligence and/or electronics surveillance; one was the son of a two-star Israeli general, and another had served as a bodyguard to the head of the Israeli army.[18]

Of the "19 Arab hijackers," 14 of them lived in South Florida at one time or another, and 12 had lived in Palm Beach County.[19] This is the very same Palm Beach County where several teams of Israeli "art students" were detained and later deported for suspicious activity.[20] Need I connect these dots for you too, or are you now seeing the picture? How appropriate that these Israeli actors should stage their stunts in a town called "Hollywood"!

These are just some of the highly suspect pieces of "evidence" that have turned up in the wake of the 9-11 attacks. ON THE OTHER HAND, nothing resembling such a phony, transparent and ridiculous trail has been found to point toward Israelis and Zionists. No Jewish skullcaps left behind at the airport, no Jewish Torahs found in "forgotten" suitcases, no six-pointed Stars of David found at crash sites, no mysterious videos of rabbis taking credit for 9-11, no Israeli passports turning up at the WTC or other crash sites, etc.

BUT THERE DOES EXIST AN ENORMOUS BODY OF REAL EVIDENCE THAT POINTS TO AN ISRAELI CONNECTION TO 9-11 AND OTHER ACTS OF TERROR AGAINST THE USA.

WHICH LEADS US TO ...

Logical Conclusion Number Six: The Muslims were framed for 9-11 by the Zionists.

Zionists and allies within the US government carried out and covered up 9-11 and the anthrax mailings. They then planted a phony evidence trail designed to frame Arabs/Muslims. Is there any other logical explanation?

Anti-Semitism, you say? Then perhaps you prefer to hear it from a Jewish scholar instead. In an article titled "The Zionist Roots of the War on Terror," Dr. Henry Makow (inventor of the board game "Scruples") writes:

> Until recently I accepted Israel's self-image as a beleaguered, peace-loving nation in a sea of blood-thirsty Arabs. The idea that this tiny state had imperialist designs seemed ludicrous. But what if, unknown to most people, including Israelis, the world's power elite were using Israel to advance their plan for New World Order? ... Israel's image of vulnerability is a ruse. Israel has always planned to become the dominant power in the region, and "invented dangers" in order to dupe its citizens and provoke wars. The Mossad's fingerprints are all over 9-11.[21]

According to Abe Foxman's and the ADL's dubious logic, Makow must therefore be a "self-hating" Jew.

22

Zionists Want to Trick America into World War III, World Crisis and World Government

In January 2001, nine months before the 9-11 attacks, a well known economist and political figure with worldwide intelligence connections issued the following prediction:

> A new Middle East war of the general type and implications indicated, will occur if certain specified incidents materialize. It will occur only if the combination of the Israeli government and certain Anglo-American circles wish to have it occur. If they should wish it to occur, the incidents to "explain" that occurrence, will be arranged.

> Contrary to widespread childish opinion, most of the important things that happen in the world, happen because powerful forces intend them to happen, not because of some so-called "sociological" or other statistical coincidence of the types reported for the popular edification of the easily

deluded. A new Middle East war, bigger than any yet seen, is inevitable under presently reigning global influences.[1]

The man who made that prediction is the perpetual presidential "wannabe" Lyndon Larouche. Larouche may be a cult-like figure with some really weird interpretations of history, but his intelligence contacts are legitimate and many of his political and economic forecasts have been accurate in the past. Considering all the history and recent events reviewed in this paper and the logical conclusions to which they lead us, the above prediction was "right on the money."

An even more chilling prophecy was issued in 1984 by Jewish author and anti-Zionist, Jack Bernstein. Bernstein warned:

> The Zionists who rule Israel and the Zionists in America have been trying to trick the US into a Mideast war on the side of Israel. They almost succeeded when US Marines were sent to Lebanon in 1982. The blood of the 250 American Marines who died in Lebanon is dripping from the hands of the Israeli and American Zionists.

> If more Americans are not made aware of the truth about Zionist Israel, you can be sure that, sooner or later, those atheists who claim to be God's Chosen People will trick the US into a Mideast war against the Arabs who in the past have always been America's best friends. Then more American boys will die because of these clever murderous Zionists, who, incidentally, have been responsible for pushing America into World War I, World War II, as well as the Korean War and Vietnam Wars. While Zionist international bankers and other Zionist Jews were busy counting their profits for those wars, American mothers and fathers, brothers and sisters were mourning the loss of their sons and brothers. Will YOU someday be mourning the loss of your son or brother—because of Zionist treachery?[2]

That part of Bernstein's warning has already come to pass. What's amazing is that Bernstein wrote that way back in 1984! But the other part of Bernstein's warning is far more chilling. Bernstein adds:

At some point during the war, when the US military is deeply involved and the US citizens are demoralized, the Zionist-oriented Jewish international bankers will make their move. Evidence leads to the conclusion that it is these bankers who own the Class A Stock of the US Federal Reserve, America's central bank. In this position of power these Zionist bankers can, and likely will, trigger an economic collapse in America—like they did in 1929 when they caused the stock market crash and started the severe depression of the 1930's.

Since the money system currently used in the US is NOT backed by gold, silver, or anything of value, the paper dollars and tin coins now in use will be worthless. In the resulting state of confusion and in an effort to obtain food and other necessities, the American people will accept the "New States Constitution" which has already been written. This will place the American people under the dictates of one-world government run by the Zionist-oriented international bankers and Zionist/Bolshevik Jews.

Exactly what direction the war in the Mideast will take only the New York/Moscow/Tel Aviv triangle and God can know. When it is all over, the main LOSERS will be: The American people. The Arab people. Those Jews who stand for justice and freedom. The only WINNERS will be: The Zionist international bankers and the Zionist/Bolshevik Jews.[3]

One has to wonder if the unusual barrage of highly publicized war movies to come out of Zionist Hollywood over the past few years was part of a propaganda effort to psychologically prepare for us for war. There was *Saving Private Ryan, Enemy at the Gates, Behind Enemy Lines, Hart's War, We Were Soldiers, Black Hawk Down, U-571, Band of Brothers*, endless TV re-runs of *The Longest Day*, and of course, the super hyped summer blockbuster of 2001 ... *PEARL HARBOR*.

The Zionists (and also other Anglo-American Internationalists) do not conceal their desire for World War Three and an eventual

New World Order (World Government), with American boys doing the dying. These are the forces that pulled off 9-11, turned us into Arab hating fanatics, put an American flag in our hands, and are marching us off to fight for Zionism. Just read what Ra'anan Gissin, a senior adviser to and spokesman for Ariel "the Butcher" Sharon, said in an interview with the *Arizona Daily Star* in April 2002:

> The terror attacks on Sept. 11 and extreme turmoil in the Middle East point to one thing—World War III. We've been fighting a war for the past 18 months, which is the harbinger of World War III. The world is going to fight, whether they like it or not. I'm sure.[4]

Here's another warmongering, inflammatory quote from Israeli Foreign Minister Shimon Peres, urging the US to attack Iraq:

> Attacking Iraq now would be quite dangerous, but postponing it would be more dangerous. The problem today is not if but when.[5]

And here's another quote from an editorial that former Israeli Prime Minister Benjamin Netanyahu wrote for the *New York Post* headlined "Today We are All Americans":

> What is at stake today is nothing less than the survival of civilization ... I have absolute confidence that if we, the citizens of the free world, led by President Bush, will marshal the enormous reserves of power at our disposal, harness the steely resolve of a free people and mobilize our collective will to eradicate this evil from the face of the earth ... The international terrorist network is thus based on regimes—Iran, Iraq, Syria, Taliban Afghanistan, Yasser Arafat's Palestinian Authority and several other Arab regimes such as the Sudan. For the bin Ladens of the world, Israel is merely a sideshow. America is the target.[6]

Note the ominous similarity between Netanyahu's lies and the first words that Sivan Kurzberg—one of the dancing Israeli "movers"—spoke to arresting police officer on 9-11: "We are Israelis. We are not your problem. Your problems are our problems. The Palestinians are your problem."[7]

Recall Netanyahu's 9-11 comment about the attacks being "very good" for Israeli-US relations. The title of the *New York Times* article that carried that comment was: "Spilled Blood is Bond That Draws 2 Nations Closer."[8]

Ariel Sharon used the same "linking tactic" in a speech before the notoriously defamatory Zionist Anti-Defamation League:

> "There is a moral equivalency and direct connection between America's continuous operations against Al-Qaeda in Afghanistan and any other Israel Defense Forces operation to defeat terrorism," Sharon said in a speech Monday to the Anti-Defamation League. "They are acts of self-defense against the same forces of evil and darkness bent on destroying civilized society."[9]

Notice how Sharon, Netanyahu, the Israeli "movers," and the totally Zionist dominated *New York Times* and *New York Post* all used the same strategic tactic of linking the interests of the US with the interests of Israel. The same ploy was utilized in the anthrax letters: "Death to America! Death to Israel!" Do see how these evil Zionist bastards play the game? They turn their enemies into our enemies while pretending to be our "allies." They laugh and celebrate as thousands of innocent Americans are burned and crushed to death. And when someone dares to shine the light of truth upon them, they label you an "anti-Semite"! Can you not see by now that these murderous swindlers have played us all for fools?

Behold this bit of bold hypocrisy by American Jewish Congress President Jack Rosen: "I don't think Palestinians celebrating the death of thousands of Americans should go unchallenged."[10]

Is that so, Jack? What about the Israelis who celebrated the death of thousands of Americans? Why haven't you challenged that?

Now read this quote from the Prince of Darkness himself—Pentagon big shot and Zionist fanatic Richard Perle:

> Neither the president nor the British Prime Minister will be deflected by Saddam's diplomatic charm offensive, the feckless moralizing of "peace" lobbies or the unsolicited advice of retired generals.[11]

Perle not only lays down the policy line for Bush, but apparently for British Prime Minister Tony Blair as well. And note how casually he dismissed the sound advice of those retired generals who warned that a war against Iraq was unnecessary. But what does Perle care! His kids won't be dying. As always, it will only be the children of the flag waving masses, which Perle and his Zionist brothers and sisters see as nothing more than cannon fodder for Zionism, who will do the fighting and killing. What threat did Iraq ever pose to the US? None! Iraq and other Arab nations are to be crushed so that Israel can expand in the Middle East while the Muslims are conquered for the New World Order.

It appears that George Bush goes along with the wishes of these Zionist gangsters for his own political protection and/or advancement, but it is unclear as to what extent he is truly in agreement with them. Bush and Cheney may even be under some form of blackmail. If not overt blackmail, just the unremitting pressure from the Christian Zionists with the GOP, the Zionist fanatics at the Pentagon, the Zionist faction in Congress, the ADL, AIPAC, the media, etc. is something that not even a US President can resist. Can you imagine what it must be like to have such pit-bulls as Foxman, Perle, Falwell, Lieberman, Robertson, and Sharon all breathing down your neck at the same time?

Bush and Cheney also represent oil interests and the Caspian Sea area is rich in oil and minerals. Plans have been in the works for years to build pipelines to take the oil from the Caspian, through Afghanistan and Pakistan and then out to sea. But the "oil angle" is but a secondary contributing factor behind the "War on Terrorism," perhaps one much nearer to the hearts of Bush/Cheney than is the cause of Zionism.

It is clear from just the well-publicized information that the President had at least some type of knowledge that a major attack was coming. Do you remember Bush's strange behavior when he was first told of the attacks? He was reading to a group of Florida school children when his Chief of Staff, Andy Card whispered the news of the second tower being hit in New York. Instead of just calmly excusing himself and apologizing to the kids for having to leave suddenly, Bush quickly shifted his eyes at the camera, turned somber, and then returned to reading for another 15 minutes![12]

Our major cities were under attack, thousands of his countrymen were burning or jumping to their deaths on live TV, and more planes were still unaccounted for. Yet Bush just sat there with a stupid look on his face and then went back to reading a story about a goat. Is this the reaction of a man who was truly surprised by these horrible attacks? Or is this more indicative of the reaction of a guilty person who, like FDR just before Pearl Harbor, was expecting an attack and therefore was not surprised?[13]

There is one more interesting coincidence worth mentioning. During the entire time that these terror attacks were expected, Bush was out of Washington DC on what the media had dubbed "the longest vacation in presidential history." *Time* magazine of August 5, 2002 explains:

> Getting ready for vacation can be so hectic. It certainly was for George W. Bush last week. While Laura Bush left the White House early to get the ranch in Crawford, Texas, ready for a month-long holiday (one of the longest in presidential history), the President rushed through last-minute errands.[14]

Bush was in Texas for the entire month of August, returned to the White House briefly, then left again and ended up in a Florida classroom on September 11. (What a tough job, eh?) Is this of any significance? Well, I don't know about you, but if I had the kind of intelligence network and advance warning that we know certain people had—and surely a sitting US president would also have had—I would not have been in Washington DC on 9-11 either!

Many politicians and journalists in America "carry the Zionists' water" for them only because they are careerists who understand very well from whence their bread is buttered. Bush has given the Zionists what they want in Iraq, but my suspicion is that if Bush doesn't deliver a total war against other Arab states, Senator Joe Lieberman may be installed as president in 2004, with his close pal John McCain running as an independent to draw votes away from Bush.

Will Bush, like Wilson in World War I, and FDR in World War II, go all the way and deliver World War III to the Zionist Mafia? It does appear that way. But if Bush should hesitate (like his father did in 1991) to "go all the way," the Zionist Mafia will likely replace him with Joe Lieberman in 2004.

Lieberman had pledged that he would defer to his 2000 ex-running mate Al Gore and not run for president if Gore had intended to. It is well known that Al Gore, who barely lost to Bush in 2000, has coveted the presidency since childhood. His father, Senator Al Gore Sr., and the late Zionist billionaire, Armand Hammer (the Gore family's chief sponsor), groomed Gore for the presidency ever since he was a little boy. Gore went into a state of near depression after losing to Bush in 2000, gaining 50 pounds and growing a thick beard! Nonetheless, the Lieberman pledge all but guaranteed that the White House-coveting Gore would not run in 2004. Higher powers surely told Gore, who would easily have won the Democratic nomination, to stand down so that Lieberman could run. It must have broken Prince Albert's heart to have announced his decision to not run, but orders are orders.

Were the Lieberman-McCain scenario to play out, the Zionist media would hype up both the Lieberman and McCain campaigns while tearing down Bush, who will have outlived his usefulness by then. Who needs a puppet when you can have the real thing? The amount of Jewish donations that would flow into Lieberman's campaign coffers would be staggering. To induce voters into sympathizing with Lieberman, expect the media to highlight the violent opposition to a Jewish candidate from the Ku Klux Klan or some odious "skin-head" group.

To insulate Lieberman from charges of first loyalty to Israel, expect some well publicized token attacks to be launched against him from pro-Israeli groups who will claim he is "too pro-Arab"! To insulate him from charges that he is a liberal, expect someone like an Al Sharpton or some Hollywood figures to attack him as "too conservative." In the public mind, this will all serve as "proof" that Lieberman is a "centrist" and an "American first" when, in reality he is an extreme tax and spend liberal and a hard core Israel Firster. The Zionists are nothing if not fiendishly clever.

It is truly saddening to think of how many innocent Iraqis (and Syrians? and Saudis? and Iranians? and Pakistanis?) will be killed and oppressed by the Zionist Pentagon military machine, with the complicity of the Zionist media. It is the media that played the key role in demonizing Iraq in the eyes of the public.

The government/media complex fabricated the lies used to justify the decade-long sanctions that have led to deaths of as many as one million Iraqis as well as the continuous bombing of Iraq. Most Americans have no idea of the true level of atrocities that have been inflicted upon the population of Iraq in our name. Instead, they are spoon-fed garbage such as George W. Bush's ridiculous response to a reporter who asked him why he thought America was hated by some Arabs. Bush replied: "Like most Americans, I just cannot believe it (that some Arabs hate us) because I know how good we are."[15]

Not a single major media commentator challenged Bush's laughable absurdity!

In the buildup to the 1991 Gulf War, the Zionist media fanned the flames of the anti-Iraq hysteria campaign by erroneously reporting that soldiers had pulled babies out of their incubators and slammed them on hospital floors during Iraq's invasion of Kuwait in 1990—a charge that was later proven false. Once the war began, the media concealed the actual number of Iraqis killed and the destruction of Iraq's infrastructure.

It is interesting to note that Jake Garner, the US General who was named to govern post-war Iraq, is openly associated with JINSA (Jewish Institute National Security Affairs).[16] Garner's office falls under the jurisdiction of arch Zionist Paul Wolfowitz, who in essence became the *de facto* ruler of post-war Iraq.[17] Oh how good 9-11 turned out to be for these "neo-conservatives"!

If "neo-conservative" guru Norman Podhoretz has his way, current US militarism in the region will escalate far beyond just the Zionist subjugation of Iraq. Writing in *Commentary* magazine, this highly influential Zionist and arrogant megalomaniac makes no attempt to conceal his desire for a World War:

> Nevertheless, there is a policy that could head it off, provided that the United States has the will to fight World War IV—the war against militant Islam—to a successful conclusion, and provided, too, that we then have the stomach to impose a new political culture on the defeated parties. This is what we did directly and unapologetically in Germany and

Japan after winning World War II.[18] [World War III was the Cold War.]

In other words, Podhoretz is saying America is just going to have to accept the fact that thousands of American boys and millions of Muslims may have to die so that we Zionists can install puppet regimes throughout the Middle East. That's exactly what the Zionists want ... and it's coming! The 9-11 attacks were the Zionists' kick-off to a major war which may in time be expanded (by design) into a truly global conflict, eventually involving nuclear powers such as India, Pakistan, North Korea, China and others. The New World Order will be built upon mountains of dead bodies and rivers of fresh blood.

In 2002, Dr. Johannes B. Koeppl, former German Defense Ministry official and advisor to former NATO Secretary General Manfred Werner, issued a dire warning about the globalist movement (in which the Zionists play a key role) and what may soon come to pass as a result of their planned global chaos. Koeppl said in an interview:

> The interests behind the Bush Administration, such as the CFR, The Trilateral Commission and the Bilderberger Group, have prepared for and are now moving to implement open world dictatorship within the next five years.

> This is more than a war against terrorism. This is a war against the citizens of all countries. The current elites are creating so much fear that people don't know how to respond. But they must remember. This is a move to implement a world dictatorship within the next five years. There may not be another chance.[19]

Iraq knew all along who was behind the "Shock and Awe" attack on their nation. In fact Harlan Ullman, the author of the "Shock and Awe" bombing strategy that was brutally unleashed upon the terrorized citizens of Iraq, is, you guessed it, a Zionist. His "Shock and Awe" catch-phrase bore an eerie similarity to the Hebrew word, "Shekinah," a popular Hebrew expression which means "the divine presence of God."

In a 2002 interview with CBS's Dan Rather, Iraqi Minister Tariq Aziz directly accused the Zionists:

> This war which the Bush government is planning does not serve the basic interest in the long run of the American nation. It serves the imperialistic interest of Israel and the Zionist groups who have now a great say in the American policy.[21]

Interestingly enough, many prominent Jewish writers agreed with Aziz! For example, in February 2003, *Time* magazine's Joe Klein wrote:

> A stronger Israel is very much embedded in the rationale for war with Iraq. It is a part of the argument that dare not speak its name, a fantasy quietly cherished by the neo-conservative faction in the Bush Administration and by many leaders of the American Jewish community.
>
> The fantasy involves a domino theory. The destruction of Saddam's Iraq will not only remove an enemy of long-standing but will also change the basic power equation in the region. It will send a message to Syria and Iran about the perils of support for Islamic terrorists. It will send a message to the Palestinians too: Democratize and make peace on Israeli terms, or forget about a state of your own.[22]

Writing for *Ha'aretz* of Israel, Jewish journalist Ari Shavit wrote:

> The war in Iraq was conceived by 25 neo-conservative intellectuals, most of them Jewish, who are pushing President Bush to change the course of history.
>
> In the course of the past year, a new belief has emerged in the town (Washington): the belief in war against Iraq. That ardent faith was disseminated by a small group of 25 or 30 neo-conservatives, almost all of them Jewish, almost all of them intellectuals (a partial list: Richard Perle, Paul Wolfowitz, Douglas Feith, William Kristol, Eliot Abrams, Charles Krauthammer), people who are mutual

friends and cultivate one another and are convinced that political ideas are a major driving force of history.[23]

And the *New York Times* Jewish columnist, Thomas Friedman stated:

> I could give you the names of 25 people (all of whom are at this moment within a five-block radius of this office) who, if you had exiled them to a desert island a year and a half ago, the Iraq war would not have happened.
>
> It is not only the neo-conservatives who led us to the outskirts of Baghdad. What led us to the outskirts of Baghdad is a very American combination of anxiety and hubris.[24]

After the fall of Baghdad, Syria and Iran became the next immediate targets of US aggression. Israel's *Ha'aretz* news service revealed that the Israeli government announced plans for an oil pipeline to run from northern Iraq through enemy Syria and into Israel, after the war was settled.[25] The fact that Syria would never allow such a pipeline to run through their territory was apparently of little consequence to the Israelis. No sooner had Israel expressed this wish for a pipeline than the Bush-Cheney-Perle-Wolfowitz-Rumsfeld crime syndicate turned its attention to Syria. No nation is safe from this criminal mob.

During the same week in which the pipeline story appeared, AIPAC held a huge convention attended by about 5,000 people. Included in attendance of the powerful Israel Lobby's affair were 1/3 of all US Congressmen and 1/2 of all US Senators![26]

According to the *Washington Post*, pro-war speakers who made threats toward Syria and Iran were cheered. In an article titled "For Israel Lobby Group, War is Topic A, Quietly," and subtitled: "At Meeting, Jerusalem's Contributions Are Highlighted," the *Post* also revealed that AIPAC was trying to keep a low profile so as not to appear that it was influencing the US war policies. (Now who would think something like that?!) Here is an excerpt from the *Post*:

> The AIPAC meeting—attended by about 5,000 people, including half the Senate and a third of the House ...
>
> A parade of top Bush administration officials—Powell, national security adviser Condoleezza Rice, political

director Kenneth Mehlman, Undersecretary of State John R. Bolton and Assistant Secretary of State William Burns— appeared before the AIPAC audience. The officials won sustained cheers for their jabs at European opponents of war in Iraq, and their tough remarks aimed at two perennial foes of Israel, Syria and Iran.

The Bush administration was somewhat ambivalent about tying itself to AIPAC and Israel. Though it sent several officials to the meeting with strong pro-Israel messages, there were efforts to keep things low-key.[27]

What other lobbying group in America can boast of having such clout? Saudi Arabia, Libya, and Muslim nuclear power Pakistan are also on the Zionist hit list. An anti-Saudi propaganda book titled *Hatred's Kingdom: How Saudi Arabia Supports the New Global Terrorism*, is being plugged incessantly by neo-conservatives and talk show stations. The author, former Israeli ambassador Dore Gold, not only spoon feeds his gullible readers the persistent lie that 15 of the 19 hijackers were Saudis, but also falsely accuses the Saudi monarchy of sponsoring anti-US terror. Meanwhile, Israel's close ally, India keeps tensions with Muslim Pakistan at dangerously high levels.

The Arabs and Muslims know too well that the Zionist Mafia dominates America. Many anti-Zionist Jews know it too. And yet, the majority of flag waving Americans are totally oblivious to this sad situation. But who will tell the American people when powerful Zionist moguls like Sumner Redstone (Viacom-CBS-MTV), Michael Eisner (ABC), Andy Lack (NBC), Norm Perlstine (*Time*), Art Sulzberger (*New York Times*), Peter Kann (*Wall Street Journal*), Mort Zuckerman (*US News & World Report, New York Daily News*), Donald Graham (*Washington Post*), Walt Isaacson (CNN), The Newhouse family (*Parade* magazine & scores of newspapers and cable stations nationwide), Spielberg/Bronfman, etc. (Hollywood), and so many other big names dominate the mass media?

23

Is America Becoming a Police State?

With the Zionist media feeding a steady diet of fear to the American public from the outside, and Zionist Senators agitating from the inside, President Bush signed the Homeland Security Department Bill and "Patriot Act" into law. The public was told that these new multi-billion dollar bureaucracies would "make us safer." Without exaggeration or hyperbole, it can truthfully be said that America's Bill of Rights has effectively been bypassed by the Homeland Security Department.

The new Homeland Security Department at the outset consists of a domestic army of 177,000 snooping Federal Bureaucrats who will be empowered to make arrests and conduct searches and surveillances without a warrant. Homeland Security will hold the power of judge, jury, and executioner all in one place—a notion that is the very antithesis of everything the American republic was founded upon.

One of America's most brilliant founders, Benjamin Franklin, forewarned of this type of creeping tyranny 200 years ago when he cautioned: "They that can give up essential liberty to obtain a little temporary safety deserve neither liberty nor safety."[1]

One of the offices empowered under the Homeland Security Department Act is the Defense Department's TIA (Office of Total Information Awareness). TIA, which was actually created in January of 2002, now gives the Zionist Pentagon the ability to track every credit card purchase you make, every phone call you make, every bank transaction, every magazine you subscribe to, and every website you visit.[2] All of the data will be stored and analyzed by computers programmed to search for certain patterns of behavior. We are told that this will help us catch "Muslim terrorists," but—if you've been paying attention—you should know by now that the domestic terror plots were not orchestrated by Muslims.

So who then are HS and the Pentagon's TIA really spying on? Look in the mirror, my friend! They will be watching YOU!

The Zionist-Federal monster knows that if World War III starts to go badly, if the draft is reinstated and the economy starts faltering, there are going to be plenty of pissed-off Americans opposing the war and asking questions. Before all hell breaks loose, Homeland Security and Total Information Awareness are aiming to put a chill on free speech and also to keep tabs on any emerging anti-government movement.

If a picture is worth a 100 words, TIA's logo tells it all. It is an image of an all-seeing eye perched on top of a pyramid and shining a bright light on planet earth.[3] Beneath the pyramid the Latin motto reads: "*Scientia Est Potentia*"—"Knowledge Is Power."

Paranoia you say? The all-seeing eyeball is TIA's logo... not mine!

It is the same pyramid and all-seeing eye that appear on the reverse side of a one-dollar bill above the Latin inscription "*Novus Ordo Seclorem*," which translates to New Order of the Ages—NEW WORLD ORDER.

The two US Senators who introduced the Homeland Security Act were Connecticut Democrat Zionist, Joe Lieberman (our next President?) and Pennsylvania Republican Zionist, Arlen Specter[4] (the inventor of the "magic bullet theory" that helped the Warren Commission cover up the truth about the Kennedy assassination).[5] And you thought there was actually a difference between the two parties!

Senator Lieberman has been a busy bee throughout this whole affair. In addition to making behind the scenes moves to prepare for a presidential run in 2004, Lieberman was the key figure behind setting up what is supposed to be an independent commission to investigate the security failures of 9-11. This was done in response to public pressure from the widows of 9-11. My dear grieving ladies! I'm sorry, but you can be sure that any "investigation" in which the hard core Zionist Joe Lieberman is involved can only result in a coverup that will make the Warren Commission report almost seem honest. I wonder if any of those Israeli "movers" and "art students" will be called to testify before the 9-11 commission anytime soon?

The man whom Bush chose to head this "investigation" (or should I say, the man Bush was told to choose!) was former Secretary of State and media darling, Henry Kissinger. Kissinger is a German-born Zionist who is a supporter and good friend of the ADL's Abe Foxman.[6] Kissinger also serves on the Pentagon's Defense Policy Board with Prince of Darkness Richard Perle. Kissinger has been manipulating US policy for 35 years. Putting "Henry the K" in charge of a 9-11 investigation is like appointing a wolf to investigate the murder of our sheep!

It didn't take long for The Group to realize this appointment was going just one step too far as the American public slowly rubs the sleep from its eyes and starts to consider the possibility that the massive amount of information now available through Internet websites and books such as this one, is actually *true*.

The pressure gauge of the masses is now registering just enough of a response to be taken into consideration. Alternative news websites, reporters and investigative journalists who write from integrity, and books such as this one, are leaking through the media and book industry barriers. Already they are having an impact on those who do not have vested interests in toeing the party line, or who are so deeply in debt they can hardly think about anything more than next month's salary.

Kissinger declined on the basis of conflict of interests.

24

Closing Arguments

We have established that the geo-political force of Zionism is a dangerous supremacist movement, and that its leaders have always placed the interests of International Zionism ahead of the interests of their respective nations. We have demonstrated that this Zionist Mafia will send unsuspecting Americans to war to fight for their interests. We have seen how Germany and Great Britain were selfishly used for their purposes.

We have demonstrated the role played by Zionism in helping to bring about some of the 20th century's greatest disasters, such as World Wars I and II and the Treaty of Versailles. We have learned about Zionist massacres of unarmed Arab civilians and Zionist terrorism designed to frame Arabs and poison relations between the US and Israel's Arab enemies.

We learned about the awesome Zionist power structure that exists in America, encompassing the Congress, the Pentagon, law enforcement, political lobbies, the mass media and more. We have established that the Zionists, through their media and book publishing dominance, have the ability to cover up and conceal some of the most amazing stories of both the past and present.

We have established a primary motive for the 9-11 attacks: to turn the US into a nation of Arab haters and Israel lovers eager to go to war against Zionism's Arab enemies and subdue those nations as well as their great mineral and oil resources, under the control of the New World Order.

We have established a secondary motive: to brutally crush the Palestinian resistance under the cover of a major US war on terrorism. With the US putting Palestine's potential protector (Saddam Hussein) permanently out of business, Israel can deal freely with the Palestinians. Sharon's tanks were unleashed on September 12 in a major escalation of the Israeli-Palestinian conflict. Because of 9-11, few even noticed and still fewer even cared.

We have established numerous precedents for these types of "false-flag" operations as well as cases of Israeli agents impersonating Arab terrorists (Lavon Affair, *USS Liberty*, Mossad agents caught with Arab passports, Taliban impersonators caught in India, belligerent Israelis in Hollywood, Florida carrying Korans inside of go-go bars, etc.).

We have established that the Zionists have the logistic capability—the means—and the opportunity to orchestrate such an operation: best intelligence service in the world, key positions of power at the Pentagon and in US intelligence, experts with explosives, access to WTC, control of security at Logan Airport and US and American Airlines, unlimited supply of money, ability to thwart investigators with phony wire translations and US moles, etc.

We have established numerous precedents which prove that the Zionist controlled media has the ability to completely cover up the shocking facts contained in this book, even after the stories had initially penetrated their own media screens. With this ability to cover up their mischief while attacking their opponents as "extremists" and "anti-Semites," there is nothing the Zionists can't get away with.

We have established that the Zionists have the power to ruin the careers of Congressmen, Senators, presidents, law enforcement officials, and journalists. Conversely, they also have the power to advance the careers of those whores who serve their interests.

We have seen that they have the ability to block investigations as well as misdirect and thwart existing investigations. We have established that the Zionists were the beneficiaries of the 9-11 attacks whereas Arabs have been hurt greatly by the 9-11 attacks.

We have exposed numerous lies linking Arabs to 9-11. We have established how evidence against Arabs was planted and contrived in order to misdirect investigators (wording of anthrax letters, phony passports, stolen passports, Korans and Arab flight manuals left conveniently behind for FBI agents to find in nightclubs, cars and "forgotten" suitcases, two hijacker passports surviving the blasts and being found, fictitious phone calls from Bin Laden to his mother, the Bin Laden "confession video" hoax, etc.). We have established that at least 7 of the 19 hijackers are alive and well. We have established that a small army of Mossad agents was caught planning terror acts in America and Mexico.

We reviewed how Zionists and their henchmen, several years before 9-11, openly wrote about how a "new Pearl Harbor" would be the only thing that could win public support for military action in the Middle East.

We have seen how anxious the Zionists were to use 9-11 as a pretext to crush the Palestinian resistance and to have the US attack Iraq and other nations.

We have established all of this and much more. In addition, there is a plethora of even more damning facts which, in the interests of time and space, were not even included in this research! The author could quite easily write additional well-researched works, each equal in size to this one, based on each sub-topic.

The only logical conclusion for a reasonable and objective person is the following:

The 9-11 attacks, the anthrax murders, the Bali bombing, the African embassy bombings and numerous other foiled terror plots, were planned, orchestrated, financed, carried out, and covered up by the forces of international Zionism.

What other logical explanation can there be? God only knows what else they have in store for us! As incredible and unthinkable as this may seem, what other conclusion is there that can so neatly tie up all of the "loose ends" and mysteries related to 9-11? This is the only scenario into which the many pieces of the 9-11 jig-saw puzzle snap snugly together to reveal a clear image.

Compare this to the official story of 9-11, which requires us to force, bend, recreate, ignore, and manipulate puzzle pieces.

Even in the face of this mountain of logic and evidence, there will be those weaklings who will go into denial and casually dismiss this whole case as just another silly "anti-Semitic conspiracy theory." But the most humorous "conspiracy theory" of all is that some Saudi caveman and his "network" of Arab video game pilots managed to elude US investigators and pull off the most sophisticated intelligence operation in world history.

You can continue to believe that fairy tale if it makes you sleep better at night (and if your sense of credulity can stand the burden!). Or, you can muster the moral and intellectual courage to free your mind from Zionist bondage and face the ugly truth. You can join the "extremists" and make a commitment to share the horrible truth with others, or, you can smirk, roll your eyes and "pooh-pooh" everything you've just read. Go back to your controlled TV news, your ballgames, your TV shows, and pretend this horror doesn't exist. Let Messrs. Rather, Brokaw, Jennings, Brown and the rest of the media whore-pack do your thinking for you while our world goes to hell in a Zionist hand-basket.

But before you go back to worshipping your favorite TV news anchor or newspaper, allow me to leave you with one last parting observation, made by the renowned Zionist propaganda specialist, Edward Bernays. Bernays, author of the book, *Propaganda*, is widely considered to be the father of modern-day advertising/public relations. He was the nephew of famed psychoanalyst, Sigmund Freud and an assistant to the Zionist William Paley, the media kingpin who founded CBS and served as its chairman for close to 50 years.

In his own words, Bernay's reveals how America is really run. Bernays wrote:

> If we understand the mechanisms and motives of the group mind, it is now possible to control and regiment the masses according to our will without their knowing it ... The conscious and intelligent manipulation of the organized habits and opinions of the masses is an important element in democratic society. Those who manipulate this unseen mechanism of society constitute an invisible government which is the true ruling power of our country ... In almost every act of our daily lives, whether in the sphere of politics

or business, in our social conduct or our ethical thinking, we are dominated by the relatively small number of persons ... who understand the mental processes and social patterns of the masses. It is they who pull the wires which control the public mind.[1]

The American public has become pawns in the Zionists' great game of global politics. Only mass exposure of this monstrous criminal activity can put a stop to it before more innocent lives are lost. A massive, international distribution of *Stranger Than Fiction* could be the key, the "Achilles heal" which can bypass Mr. Bernay's controlled media and shake this planet to its very foundations.

The choice is yours. History and posterity will judge your actions—or inactions—accordingly.

To borrow a line from Maximus, hero of the film *Gladiator*: "What we do in life, echoes in eternity."

Reader, what will you do?

A Closing Statement from the Father of Our Country

A passionate attachment of one nation for another produces a variety of evils. Sympathy for the favorite nation, facilitating the illusion of an imaginary common interest in cases where no real common interest exists, and infusing into one nation the enmities of the other, betrays the former into a participation in the quarrels and wars of the latter without justification. It leads also to concessions to the favorite nation of privileges denied to others which is apt doubly to injure the nation making the concessions; by unnecessarily parting with what ought to have been retained, and by exciting jealousy, ill-will, and a disposition to retaliate, in the parties from whom equal privileges are withheld. And it gives to ambitious, corrupted, or deluded citizens who devote themselves to the favorite nation, facility to betray or sacrifice the interests of their own country.

—George Washington[1]

Endnotes and Key Search Words for Yahoo or www.google.com

CHAPTER 2

1. Athens *Banner-Herald*, December 22, 2001. Google users, enter these words: university chicago poll americans cried.
2. *Yediot America* (Israeli Newspaper), November 2, 2001. Google users, enter: yediot america urban moving.
3. *Ha'aretz*, September 17, 2001. 5 Israelis detained for "puzzling behavior" after WTC tragedy.
4. *Jewish Week*, November 2, 2001. Stewart Ain. Google users, enter: urban moving Israelis smiling took pictures on 9-11.
5. ABC News-*20/20*. ABCNews.com, June 21, 2001. Google users, enter : white van Israeli spies.
6. *Bergen Record* [New Jersey], September 12, 2001. Paolo Lima. Google users, enter: Bergen Lima five Israelis.

CHAPTER 3

1. *Eye For An Eye*, by John Sack. Google users, enter: john sack eye for eye.
2. *The Zionist Connection*, by Alfred Lilienthal. Google users, enter: alfred lilienthal Zionist.

3. "Fateful Triangle," by Noam Chomsky. Google users, enter: chomsky fateful triangle.
4. "Open Secrets," by Israel Shahak. Google users, enter: israel shahack open secrets.
5. "The Hidden Tyranny," by Benjamin Freedman. Google users, enter: benjamin freedman.
6. *The Life Of An American Jew In Racist-Marxist Israel,* by Jack Bernstein, © 1984.
7. "The Zionist Roots Of The 'War On Terror' Israel's Policy Of 'Covert Aggression,'" by Dr. Henry Makow. www.savethemales.com. November 2002.
8. *By Way of Deception,* by Victor Ostrovsky. Google users, enter: victor ostrovsky.
9. *Neturei Karta*-Jews United Against Zionism. Google users, enter: neturei karta jews against Zionism.
10. *The Life Of An American Jew In Racist-Marxist Israel,* by Jack Bernstein, © 1984.
11. *The New Freedom,* Woodrow Wilson, 1913. Google users, enter: new freedom some of biggest men afraid.
12. Jewish Virtual Library of the American-Israeli co-operative enterprise. Google users, enter: weizmann balfour Zionist.
13. Benjamin Freedman's 1955 speech. Google users, enter: Benjamin Freedman speaks, and also: Benjamin Freedman.
14. *Square One: A Memoir,* by Arnold Forster. Google users, enter: Arnold Forster Square One. . . . or see amazon.com.
15. Same as #13.
16. *Microsoft Encarta Encyclopedia,* "Balfour Declaration." Google users, enter: Balfour Zionism.

CHAPTER 4

1. "Judea Declares War on Germany." *Daily Express* (UK), March 24, 1933. Google users, enter: Judea Declares War on Germany.
2. "Vladimir Jabotinsky," by Mascha Rjetsch, January, 1934. Google users, enter: vladimir jabotinsky and also jabotinsky mascha rjetsch.

3. Beaverbrook papers. House of Lords Records Service. (England). Google users, enter: beaverbrook jews position press.
4. Charles Lindbergh's Speech in Iowa. September 11, 1941. Google users, enter: Lindbergh Des Moines speech.
5. *Day of Deceit,* by Robert Stinnett. Google users, enter: day of deceit stinnett.
6. From Adolf Hitler's last Will and Political Testament. Google users, enter: Hitler my political testament.

CHAPTER 5

1. Britain's Small Wars. Google users, enter: dressed as Arabs king david and also king david hotel bombing.
2. Deir Yassin Remembered. Google users, enter: deir Yassin remembered and also deir Yassin.
3. "Conscience and the Dilemma of Zionism," by Hannah Arendt. The American Council for Judaism. Keith Morrison Issues, Summer 1995. Google users, enter: hannah arendt conscience dilemma Zionism.
4. Ibid.
5. The Khazaria Information Center. Google users, enter: Khazars.

CHAPTER 6

1. *By Way of Deception,* by Victor Ostrovsky. Google users, enter: mossad motto.
2. *The Gun and the Olive Branch,* by David Hirst. Google users, enter: lavon affair.
3. *Assault on Liberty,* by James M Ennes Jr. Google users, enter: ennes uss liberty.
4. "How Mossad got America to bomb Libya and fight Iraq," by Victor Ostrovsky. Google users, enter: ostrovsky how mossad got america.

5. "The Contrasting Media Treatment of Israeli and Islamic Death Threats," by Victor Ostrovsky. Google users, enter: Ostrovsky death threats.
6. "Army Study Suggests US Force of 20,000," by Rowan Scarborough. The *Washington Times*, September 10, 2001. Google users, enter: army study suggests sams rowan scarborough.
7. Ibid.

CHAPTER 7

1. *The International Jew*, by Henry Ford. Google users, enter: ford international jew.
2. "Lindbergh and the Jews" by Hal Derner. *Jewish Frontier*. Google users, enter: lindbergh jews press.
3. "They Dare to Speak Out," by Paul Findley. Google users, enter: admiral moorer boggles mind.
4. Senator William Fulbright on ABC's *Face the Nation*. Google users, enter: fulbright israel controls senate.
5. Patrick Buchanan on the Mclaughlin Group. Google users, enter: buchanan israeli occupied territory.
6. Rev. Billy Graham and Richard Nixon. CNN Google users, enter: graham jewish media stranglehold.
7. "Passionate Attachment to Israel," by General James J. David. Media Monitors Network.
8. *Who Rules America?* by Dr. William Pierce. Google users, enter: jewish media control.
9. "The Israel Lobby," by Michael Massing. *The Nation* magazine. Google users, enter: massing israel lobby.
10. "Saudis Lash Out at 'Zionist' US Critics," by Marc Perelman. *Jewish Forward*. Google users, enter: forward zionist defense policy board.
11. CNN, March 16, 2002. Novak, Hunt, and Shields.
12. Ari Shavit, *Ha'aretz*, reprinted in *New York Times*. May 27 1996. Google users, enter: sobran shavit in our hands.
13. "Bubba: I'd fight and Die for Israel," by Andy Geler, *New York Post*. August 2, 2002. Google users, enter: clinton grab a rifle fight die.

CHAPTER 8

1. CNN, "Rabin Assassinated at Peace Rally," November 4, 1995. Google users, enter: rabin assassinated.
2. BBC News, "Clinton Sorry for Lewinsky Affair," September 4, 1998.
3. "The Fateful Triangle," Noam Chomsky's Account of the Sabra and Shatila Massacre. Google users, enter: Chomsky Sabra Shatila.
4. "Third former Militiaman with Links to Sabra and Chatila Murdered," By Robert Fisk. *The Independent*, March 11, 2001. Google users, enter: fisk former militiaman murdered.
5. CNN. Israeli troops, Palestinians clash after Sharon visits Jerusalem sacred site. September 28, 2002. Google users, enter: cnn after sharon visits sacred.
6. "Why we refuse to Fight," by Rami Kaplan. *Counterpunch*, May 2, 2002. Google: why we refuse to fight rami Kaplan.

CHAPTER 9

1. India Reacts. India in anti-Taliban military plan. June 21, 2001. Google users, enter: india anti taliban military plan.
2. Ibid.
3. "India joins anti-Taliban coalition," by Rahul Bedi. Jane's International Security News. (England), March 15, 2001. Google users, enter: india joins anti-taliban coalition Rahul Bedi.
4. *ABC Nightline* with Ted Koppel. March 10, 2003. The Plan: Were Neo-Conservatives' 1998 Memos a Blueprint for War? Google: Project new american century new pearl harbor.
5. "Israeli security issued urgent warning to CIA of large-scale terror attacks," by David Wastell in Washington and Philip Jacobson in Jerusalem. *The Telegraph* (England), September 16, 2001. Google users, enter: telegraph israeli security issued urgent warning.
6. "Echelon Gave Authorities Warning Of Attacks," by Ned Stafford. "Biz Report" from *Frankfurter Allgemeine Zeitung*

(Germany) September 13, 2001. Google users, enter: Zeitung of Germany Echelon Gave Authorities Warning.
7. Ibid.
8. "Willie Brown got low-key early warning about air travel," by Phillip Matier, Andrew Ross. *San Francisco Chronicle*, September 12, 2001. Google users, enter: chronicle willie brown got early warning.
9. "Bush: We're at War," by Evan Thomas and Mark Hosenball. *Newsweek*, September 24, 2001. Google users, enter: newsweek bush evan thomas we're at war.
10. "Instant message to Israel warned of WTC attack," by Brian McWiliams. "Newsbytes" - *Washington Post*, September 27, 2001. Google users, enter: instant messages Israel warned attack.

CHAPTER 10

1. "Spilled Blood is Seen as Bond That Draws 2 Nations Closer," by James Bennet. *New York Times*, September 12, 2001. Google users, enter: it will generate immediate sympathy for Israel.
2. *NBC News*. Exclusive: 9/11 Tapes Tell Horror Of 9/11 Tapes Released For First Time UPDATED: 5:48 p.m. EST June 17, 2002. Google users, enter: look like Palestinians and going around a building.
3. ABC News - *20/20*. ABCNews.com, June 21, 2001.Google users, enter : white van Israeli spies.
4. "Five Men Detained as Suspected Conspirators," by Paulo Lima. The *Bergen Record* (New Jersey), September 12, 2001. Google users, enter: paulo lima five men detained.
5. "Car Bomb found on George Washington Bridge." *Jerusalem Post*, September 12, 2001.
6. See #3.
7. http://www.whatreallyhappened.com/forget.html, *New York Post* article by Al Guart, September 13, 2001.
8. See #4.

9. http://www.whatreallyhappened.com/forget.html. *Arutz*, Israeli National News, 10-26-01.

10. *Yediot America* (Israeli Newspaper), November 2, 2001. Google users, enter: yediot america urban moving.

11. "Five hijack suspects had links to N.J.," by Adam Lisberg. The *Bergen Record* (New Jersey), September 15, 2001. Google users, enter: adam lisberg guys were joking.

12. New Jersey Department of Law and Public Safety. Division of Consumer Affairs. December 13, 2001. Google users, enter: state granted access to moving facility.

13. "Spy Rumors Fly on Ghosts of Truth," by Marc Perelman. The *Forward*, March 15, 2001. Google users, enter: Americans Probing Reports of Israeli Espionage.

14. ABC News - *20/20*. ABCNews.com, June 21, 2001. Google users, enter: white van Israeli spies.

15. *Unmat* (Pakistan). From BBC Monitoring Service. September 28, 2001. Google users, enter: bin laden already said I am not involved.

CHAPTER 11

1. WCBV TV. Boston Channel. FBI Agents Search Hotels; Several People Detained, September 12, 2001. Google users, enter: boston airport koran arab flight.

2. Ibid.

3. "Uncle Sam's Lucky Finds," by Anne Karpf. *Guardian Unlimited* (England). March 19, 2002. Google users, enter: uncle sam lucky finds anne karpf and also atta passport found.

4. "September 11 hijacker questioned in January 2001," by David Ensor and Sheila McVickers. CNN.com - August 1, 2002.

5. ABCNews.com. "Saudi Prince says Seven Saudis on FBI list Innocent," September 23, 2001. Google users, enter: hijack suspects alive and well.

6. "Revealed: The Men With Stolen Identities," by David Harrison. The *Telegraph* (England), September 23, 2001.

Google users, enter: hijackers still alive and well and also
telegraph men with stolen identities hijackers.

7. ABC - ABCNews.com. "Saudi Prince says Seven Saudis on FBI
list Innocent," September 23, 2001. Google users, enter: hijack
suspects alive and well.
8. "Hijack Suspects alive and well." BBC News (England), September
23, 2001. Google users, enter: hijack suspects alive and well.
9. "Hijackers likely skilled with fake IDs," CNN, September 21,
2001. Google users, enter: cnn mueller identity thefts.
10. "Some Hijacker Identities Uncertain," by Dan Eggen,
George Lardner Jr. and Susan Schmidt. *Washington Post*,
September 20, 2001.
11. "Aborted Mission Investigation: Did Mossad attempt to infiltrate Islamic radical outfits in south Asia?" by Subir Bhaumik.
The Week (India), February 6, 2000. Google users, enter:
muslim tabliqis Mossad.
12. Indian intelligence wiretap identified 9/11 hijackers. *Express
India, Press Trust of India*, April 3, 2002. Google users, enter:
indian intelligence wiretap identified 9/11.
13. "Israel's New Best Friend?" by Gil Sedan. *Jewsweek*. India, The
Jewish Telegraph Agency. August 2002. Google users, enter: jewsweek Israel new best friend.
14. Wikipedia.com. *The Free Encyclopedia*. Mohammed Atta.
Google users, enter: atta reported passport stolen.
15. *Frontline*, PBS. "Inside the Terror network," January 17, 2002.
Google users, enter: frontline atta shy timid.
16. "A Mission To Die For," Rudi Dekkers interviewed by Quentin
McDermott. ABC Channel 4. (Florida), October 21, 2001
Google users, enter: rudi dekkers interview.
17. Ibid.
18. Ibid.
19. "Eagan Flight Trainer Won't Let Unease about Moussaoui
Rest," *Star Tribune*, December 21, 2001. Google users, enter: star
tribune eagan flight trainer.
20. "He Never Even Had a Kite," by Alan Zarembo. MSNBC,
September 24, 2001. Google users, enter: atta he never even
had kite.

21. "The Israeli Art Student Papers," by Justin Raimondo. Antiwar.com. March 21, 2002. Google users, enter: Israeli art students Hollywood.
22. *Boston Globe*, March 5, 1994. Google users, enter: baruch goldstein.
23. Goldstein memorial website. http://www.newkach.org/special/baruch/02.htm. Google users, enter: baruch Goldstein.
24. "JDL's Irv Rubin Brain Dead After Suicide Attempt," by Dan Whitcomb. *Reuters*.
25. "At least two Israelis dead in Tower attack," by Mazal Mualem and Shlomo Shamir. *Ha'aretz* (Israel). Google users, enter: daniel lewin elite commando.

CHAPTER 12

1. "Investigators Arrive at Payne Stewart Crash Site," CNN, October 26, 1999. Google users, enter: CNN payne stewart crash.
2. "Defensive Saudis Lash Out at 'Zionist' and US Critics," by Marc Perelman. *Forward*. December 28, 2001. Google users, enter: perle zionist defense policy board.
3. "Bush: We're at War," by Evan Thomas and Mark Hosenball. *Newsweek*, September 24, 2001. Google users, enter: newsweek bush evan thomas we're at war.
4. Interview with General Gul, UPI United Press International. September 26, 2001. Google users, enter: hamid gul upi interview.
5. "Former Top German Spy Says US Wrong About September 11," by Christopher Bollyn. The *American Free Press*, Jan 28, 2002, quoting from *Tagesspiegel* interview, published on Jan. 13, 2002. Google users, enter: andreas von bulow interview.
6. "Conspiracy Theories Arise From September 11 Attacks," by James Rosen McClatchy. Washington Bureau 1-13-2. *Fresno Bee* - "Analysis." Google: "Let us never tolerate outrageous conspiracy theories."
7. "David Frum's Guide to Mythology," by Christopher Montgomery, October 30, 2002. Airstrip One (England), antiwar.com.

8. "United States Calls Sharon a Man of Peace," by Randell Mikkelson. *Reuters*, April 11, 2002.
9. Press release from Law Firm of Baum, Hedlund, Aristei, Guilford & Schiavo, April 11, 2002. Google users, enter: family members lawsuit huntleigh 9-11.
10. Ibid.
11. Hoover's Online - The Business Information Authority. Google users, enter: hoover online icts.
12. "Experience, Reputation Make Israelis Hot Commodities for Homeland Security," by John P. Mcalpin. *Associated Press*, March 21, 2002. Google users, enter: mcalpin experience reputation make Israelis.
13. "Hackers using Israeli 'net site to strike at Pentagon,' " by Nitzan Horowitz. *Ha'aretz* (Israel), July 30, 1999. Google users, enter: Israel hackers pentagon.
14. US Department of Justice Press Release, March 18, 1998. Google users, enter: israeli citizen arrested israel hacking.

CHAPTER 13

1. "WTC Architect: Collapse 'Unbelievable,' " by Michael Meyer and Stuart Winer. *Jerusalem Post*, September 12, 2001. Google users, enter: swirsky collapse unbelievable.
2. "Eyewitness Reports Persis Of Bombs At WTC Collapse," by Christopher Bollyn. *American Free Press*, December 12, 2001. Google users, enter: bollyn bombs lee Robertson.
3. "Explosives planted in towers, N.M. Tech Expert Says," by Oliver Uyttebrouck. *Albuquerque Journal*. ABQjournal.com, September 11, 2001. Google users, enter: romero explosives planted tower.
4. "Fire, Not Extra Explosives, Doomed Buildings, Expert Says," by John Fleck. *Albuquerque Journal*. ABQjournal.com, September 21, 2001. Google users, enter: van romero fire not explosives.
5. "United in Courage," *People* Magazine. People.com, September 12, 2001. Google users, enter: people louie cacchioli 51.

6. "World Trade Center Scrap Sails for India, China," by Pete Harrison and Manuela Badawy. *Reuters*, January 21, 2002. Google users, enter: world trade center scrap sails.

7. Chinese Radio International, January 2002. Google users, enter: cri online world centre trade scrap.

8. "Firefighter Mag raps 9/11 Probe," by Joe Calderone. *New York Daily News*, January 4, 2002. Google users, enter: joe calderone firefighter mag raps.

9. Ibid.

10. "Experts Urging Broader Inquiry In Towers' Fall," *New York Times*, December 25, 2001. Google users, enter: times experts urging broader inquiry towers fall.

11. Ibid.

12. Ibid.

CHAPTER 14

1. "Census of Sept. 11 Victims," by Birthplace. *News India*, April 26, 2002. Google users, enter: census of Sept. 11 victims by birthplace.

2. "Thousands of Israelis missing near WTC, Pentagon." *Jerusalem Post*, September 12, 2002. Google users, enter: jerusalem post thousands israelis missing.

3. "Bush speech to US Congress," *New York Times*, September 22, 2001. Google users, enter: nor will we forget more than 130 israelis.

4. "September 11: A Memorial," CNN. Google users, enter: cnn september 11 memorial.

5. *New York Times*, September 22, 2001.

6. "Instant message to Israel warned of WTC attack. September 27, 2001," by Brian McWiliams. "Newsbytes" - *Washington Post*. Google users, enter: instant messages Israel warned attack.

7. "Zim Workers Saved By Cost-Cutting Measures," *Jerusalem Post Digital Israel*, November 12, 2001. Google users, enter: zim workers saved if removed try: zim saved by move to virginia zim Israel navigation.

8. "Zim saved by a Move to Virginia," *Bible Light International*, June 2001. Google users, enter: zim israel navigation world trade center Virginia.
9. "Zim Workers Saved By Cost-Cutting Measures," *Jerusalem Post Digital Israel*, November 12, 2001. Google users, enter: zim workers saved if removed try: zim saved by move to virginia zim Israel navigation.
10. "Zim saved by a Move to Virginia," *Bible Light International*, June 2001. Google users, enter: zim israel navigation world trade center Virginia.
11. "Zim Workers Saved By Cost-Cutting Measures," *Jerusalem Post Digital Israel*, November 12, 2001. Google users, enter: zim workers saved if removed try: zim saved by move to virginia zim Israel navigation.
12. "Zim saved by a Move to Virginia," *Bible Light International*, June 2001. Google users, enter: zim israel navigation world trade center Virginia.

CHAPTER 15

1. "India in anti-Taliban military plan," *India Reacts*, June 21, 2001. Google users, enter: india anti taliban military plan.
2. "India joins anti-Taliban coalition," by Rahul Bedi. *Jane's International Security News* (England), March 15, 2001. Google users, enter: india joins anti-taliban coalition Rahul Bedi.
3. *Der Erste* (Germany) Monitor, aired December 20, 2001 [Translated by Craig Morris]. Google users, enter: bin laden translation manipulated for German original transcripts enter: monitor bin laden video restle sieker.
4. Ibid.
5. Sam Lacey, "More Osama Video Analysis." Google users, enter: more osama video analysis.
6. "Pentagon Considers Using Lies," by James Dao & Eric Schmitt. *The New York Times*, February 18, 2001. Google users, enter: new york times simon worden osi.

7. Zionist Organization of America Press Release, October 13, 1997. Google users, enter: Zionist organization america feith award.
8. "Asteroid could start nuke war," by Richard Stenger. CNN. General, Thursday, October 3, 2002.
9. "FBI Fails to Expose al-Qaeda networks," by Daniel McGrory. *The Times* (England), March 11, 2002. Google users, enter: FBI Fails Expose al-Qaeda networks.
10. "The Plot thins as FBI hunts for evidence," *Sydney Morning Herald*, May 1, 2002 (Reprinted from *Los Angeles Times*). Google users, enter: plot thins as FBI hunts evidence.

CHAPTER 16

1. "2 Found with Video of Swears Tower," by Michelle Mowad. *The Mercury* (Philadelphia area newspaper), October 17, 2001. Google users, enter: Mercury 2 found video sears tower.
2. Ibid.
3. Ibid.
4. Ibid.
5. "Bomba en San Lazaro," *Diario de Mexico*, October 11, 2001. Google users, enter: action report visual proof mexico and also mossad terrorists mexico.
6. Mexican Department of Justice, (PGR) Press Bulletin. October 12, 2001. Bulletin 697/01. PGR bulletin can be viewed in Spanish; Google users, enter: Mossad terrorists penetrate Mexican congress.
7. "Bomba en San Lazaro," *Diario de Mexico*, October 11, 2001. Google users, enter: action report visual proof mexico and also mossad terrorists mexico.
8. "Mexican Attorney General Releases Zionist Terrorists," by Ernesto Cienfuegos. *La Voz de Aztlan*, October 15, 2001. Google users, enter: mossad zionist terrorists mexico.
9. "Army General and Head of the PGR Releases Two Israelis Arrested With Guns and Explosives Inside the Mexican

Congress," by Ernesto Cienfuegos. *La Voz de Aztlan*, October 15, 2001.

10. "FBI suspect Israelis of Nuclear Terrorism," *Jerusalem Post*, November 1, 2001. Go to: ww.jpost.com/Editions/2001/11/01/ LatestNews/LatestNews.37390.html (Case sensitive; enter lower case and upper case letters exactly as shown) or Google to: Jerusalem post FBI suspect israelis nuclear.

11. Ibid.

12. "Nuclear plants tighten security FBI seeking 6 men seen in Midwest," by Martin Merzer, Curtis Morgan, & Lenny Savino. *Miami Herald*, October 3, 2001. Google users, enter: miami herald israelis nuclear power plans.

13. "FBI Fury as Men with Nuclear Plan Escape," by Katty Kay in Washington. *The Times* (England), November 1, 2001. Google users, enter: katty kay fbi nuclear plan Israeli.

14. "Militant JDL Members Arrested by FBI," by Linda Deutsch. *Los Angeles Times*, December 12, 2001. Google users, enter: jdl bomb rubin issa.

15. "Police Seize Rental Truck with TNT Traces," by Carl Cameron. FOX News, May 13, 2001. Google users, enter: fox bomb sniffing Israeli truck.

16. "Two Israelis wanted in US After Traces of Explosives Found in Their Truck," *Ha'aretz* (Israel), May 18, 2002. Google users, enter: american police arrested two Israelis gear shift. NEW.

17. "Palestinians Arrest Israeli Poseurs," *Sydney Morning Herald* (Australia), December 8, 2002.

18. "Massive Israeli Spy Operation 2 Discovered in US: Carl Cameron Investigates - Four Part series," by Carl Cameron. *FOX News*, December 2001. Google users, enter: israeli spy carl cameron investigates.

19. "60 Israelis on Tourist Visas detained Since Sept. 11," by John Mintz. *Washington Post*, November 23, 2001. Google users, enter: washington post 60 Israelis detained.

20. "Carl Cameron Investigates. This Story No Longer Exists." FOX News website, December 21, 2001. View this very strange

posting . . . Google users, enter: carl cameron this story no longer exists. http://www.foxnews.com/story/0,2933,40684,00.html.

21. "Massive Israeli Spy Operation 2 Discovered in US: Carl Cameron Investigates - Four Part series," by Carl Cameron. *FOX News*, December 2001. Google users, enter: israeli spy carl cameron investigates.

22. "Federal Buildings Could be in Jeopardy" KHOU, Channel 11 (Houston) - in Houston and Nationally October 1, 2001. Google users, enter: israeli art students federal buildings.

23. Ibid.

24. "Fifteen People Arrested in March in Dallas, Suspected of Casing Federal Buildings," by Anna Werner. KHOU, Google: Fifteen People Arrested in March in Dallas, Suspected of Casing Federal Buildings.

25. "ADL tracks Growth of Militia Movement." ADL Press Release, June 19, 1995.

26. "Massive Israeli Spy Operation Discovered in US: Carl Cameron Investigates - Four Part series," by Carl Cameron. *FOX News*, December 2001. Google users, enter: Israeli spy carl Cameron.

27. See Chapter 9, Footnote #4.

28. See Chapter 15, Footnotes #9 and #10.

29. "Massive Israeli Spy Operation Discovered in US: Carl Cameron Investigates - Four Part series," by Carl Cameron. *FOX News*, December 2001. Google users, enter: Israeli spy carl Cameron.

30. "La Guardia Airport evacuated," by Cap 9 Staff. Capital 9 News (Albany, New York), March 22, 2003. Internet: http://www.whatreallyhappened.com/laguardia.html.

31. "Powdery substance found at New York's La Guardia," *Reuters*, March 21, 2003. Internet: http://www.whatreallyhappened.com/laguardia.html.

32. "Suspicious Substance Probed At La Guardia," by Joshua Robin. *New York Newsday*, March 21, 2003. Internet: http://www.whatreallyhappened.com/laguardia7.htm.

33. "Improving Intelligence," *PBS Newshour*, December 11, 2002.

34. Op. cit., #21.

CHAPTER 17

1. "The Counter-Terrorist: John O'Neill was an F.B.I. agent with an obsession: the growing threat of Al-Qaeda," by Lawrence Wright. *New Yorker* magazine, Jan. 14, 2002.
2. "Scandal inside the FBI: Why did G-Men Miss the Boat on 9-11?" by Wes Vernon. *Newsmax*, March 14, 2002. Google users, enter: robert wright fbi.
3. "FBI Called off Terror Investigations," by Brian Ross and Vic Walter. ABC News.com, December 19, 2002.
4. Ibid.
5. Ibid.
6. "Coleen Rowley's Memo to FBI Director Robert Mueller," *Time* magazine. Time.com. May 21, 2002. Google users, enter: time rowley memo Mueller.
7. Ibid.
8. "Two FBI whistleblowers Allege Lax Security, Possible Espionage," by James V. Grimaldi. *Washington Post*, June 18, 2001. Google users, enter: sibel edmunds john cole.
9. Ibid.
10. Ibid.
11. "Inquiries of Intelligence failures Hits Obstacles," by Greg Miller. *Los Angeles Times*. Google users, enter: times inquiry intelligence failures hits.
12. "Keeping Score in the Great Game of Politics: Senators lobby for resignation of CIA Director," EVOTE.COM, September 13, 2002.
13. "Senator wants FBI to explain bonus for official in 9/11 case," by Jerry Seper. *Washington Times*, January 11, 2002.

CHAPTER 18

1. "New Excuses, Old Hatred: Worldwide Anti-Semitism In Wake Of 9/11," by Abraham H. Foxman, National Director of the Anti-Defamation League. Google: foxman anti Zionism is anti Semitism.
2. Ibid.

3. FBI Major Speeches-Anti-Defamation League's 24th Annual National Leadership Conference, Washington, DC. May 7, 2002. www.fbi.gov. Google users, enter: Mueller fbi adl speech.
4. 2000 Annual Report, Anti-Defamation League. Google users, enter: tenet adl.
5. Ibid.
6. Ibid.
7 Ibid.
8. ADL Report, Tuesday, May 1, 2001. Google users, enter: Ashcroft ADL Leadership Conference.
9. "ADL Found Guilty Of Spying By California Court," by Barbara Ferguson, *Arab News* Correspondent. *Arab News,* April 27, 2002. Google users, enter: barbara Ferguson adl guilty.
10. Ibid.
11. "Blame the Terrorists, Not Israel," ADL Press Release, September 21, 2001.

CHAPTER 19

1. "Turmoil in a Perilous Place: Angry Scientists Allege Racism at Bio-warfare Lab," by Lynee Tuohy & Jack Dolan. *Hartford Courant,* December 19, 2001. Google users, enter: courant assaad zack anthrax.
2. Ibid.
3. FBI. www.fbi.gov. Google users, enter: anthrax letters.
4. Ibid.
5. "Turmoil in a Perilous Place: Angry Scientists Allege Racism at Biowarfare Lab," by Lynee Tuohy & Jack Dolan. *Hartford Courant.* December 19, 2001. Google users, enter: courant turmoil perilous place. Also: anthrax downs zack.
6. Ibid.
7. Ibid.
8. "Anthrax Missing from Army Lab," by Jack Dolan & Dave Altimari. *Hartford Courant.* January 20, 2001. Google users, enter: courant anthrax missing army lab.
9. Ibid.

10. See footnotes 165 and 166.
11. "On the Trail of an Anthrax Killer," by Paul Koring. *Globe and Mail* (Canada), March 6, 2001. Google users, enter: globe mail trail anthrax killer.
12. "Deadly specimens disappeared from Army research lab in '90s," *Seattle Times* (Reprinted from *Hartford Courant*), January 21, 2002. Google users, enter: seattle times anthrax zack.
13. "Media Manufacture Cloud of Suspicion Over Hatfill," by Nicholas Stix. *Insight* magazine, August 14, 2002. Google users, enter: kristof hatfill.
14. "Expert: Anthrax Suspect ID'd," by Joseph Dee. *The Times of Trenton*. February 19, 2002. Google users, enter: rosenberg Hatfill.
15. "Media Manufacture Cloud of Suspicion Over Hatfill," by Nicholas Stix. *Insight* magazine. August 14, 2002. Google users, enter: kristof hatfill
16. "Ex-Army Scientist Denies Role in Anthrax Attacks," *Washington Post*, August 2002. Google users, enter: rosenberg Hatfill.
17. "Scientist Says FBI asked About Setup," by Gus Taylor. August 3, 2001. *Washington Times*. Google users, enter: hatfill fbi passed lie detector test.

CHAPTER 20

1. "COMMENTARY: Evangelical Christians and the Sharon lobby," by Jim Lobe. *Asia Times Online*, April 27, 2002.
2. patrobertson.com, July 10, 2002.
3. CBN. The 700 Club. 1997.

CHAPTER 21

1. Unmat (Pakistan), from BBC Monitoring Service, September 28, 2001. Google users, enter: bin laden already said I am not involved.
2. See Chapter 9, Footnote #4.

3. "Sources dispute reports of bin Laden phone call," by David Ensor and Eileen O'Connor, CNN National Security Correspondent. CNN.com, October 2, 2001. Google: Sources dispute reports of Bin laden phone call mother.

4. "The investigation and the evidence," BBC News - AMERICAS, Friday, October 5, 2001. Google: BBC the investigation and the evidence.

5. "Airline denied Atta paradise wedding suit," by Paul Sperry. *WorldNet Daily*. September 11, 2001.

6. "Handwritten Letter Instructed Hijackers Words of Terror: Handwritten Letter Gave Hijackers Religious, Practical Instructions," ABCNEWS.com, Sept. 28, 2001.

7. "What Did Happen to Flight 93?" Richard Wallace, US Editor, examines riddle of hijacked jet as he visits crash site, *Mirror* (UK), December 2001.

8. "Giuliani holds on to hope," BBC News: AMERICAS, September 16, 2001. Google: BBC Giuliani holds on to hope.

9. BBC, Monday, 19 November, 2001, Hijacker's Farewell Love Letter.

10. See Chapter 11, footnotes #8 and #9.

11. See Chapter 11, footnotes #5, #6, and #7.

12. See Chapter 18, Footnote #8.

13. See Chapter 15, Footnotes #3, #4, and #5.

14. "US says Card Links Mouassaoui, Hijackers," by Tom Jackman. *Washington Post*, September 25, 2002.

15. "September 11 hijacker questioned in January 2001," by Sheila MacVicar and Caroline Faraj. CNN.com, August 1, 2002.

16. "FBI tracks down the Florida lair of flying school terrorists," by Ian Ball in Miami. *The Telegraph* (UK). Google: Mohammed Atta vodka Hollywood.

17. "Focus On Florida," by Brendan Farrington. MMI *Associated Press. CBS News*, September 14, 2001, 08:22:41.

18. "The Israeli "art student" mystery," by Christopher Ketchum, *Salon* magazine, May 7, 2002. Salon.com News. Google: salon magazine Israeli art student mystery.

19. "14 hijackers spent time in Florida," by Barry Klein, Wes Allison, David Adams and Kathryn Wexsler. *St. Petersburg*

Times, September 15, 2001. Google: 14 hijackers spent time florida.

20. "Investigative Report. Intelligence Agents Or Art Students?" by Paul M. Rodriguez. *Insight* magazine. March 11, 2002.

21. "The Zionist Roots of the War on Terror," Dr. Henry Makow, November 18, 2001. www.savethemales.ca.

CHAPTER 22

1. "Executive Intelligence Review," Lyndon Larouche, January 2001. Google users, enter: larouche middle east war implications.

2. *The Life Of An American Jew In Racist-Marxist Israel,* by Jack Bernstein, 1984.

3. Ibid.

4. "World War III Is Coming 'Whether They Like It Or Not' - Top Sharon Aide," by Stephanie Innes. *Arizona Daily Star,* April 27, 2002. Google users, enter: gissin world war coming like or not.

5. "Israel to US: Don't Wait To Attack Iraq, Report Says," *CNS News.* August 2002. Google users, enter: peres iraq attack.

6. "Today We are All Americans," by Benjamin Netanyahu. *New York Post,* September 21, 2001. Google users, enter: netanyahu today we all Americans.

7. *ABC News - 20/20.* ABCNews.com, June 21, 2001.Google users, enter: white van Israeli spies.

8. "Spilled Blood is Seen as Bond That Draws 2 Nations Closer," by James Bennet. *New York Times,* September 12, 2001. Google users, enter: new york times spilled blood bond draws.

9. "Sharon Compares Incursions to US War on Terror," CNN.com. May 7, 2002. Google users, enter: Sharon speech adl.

10. "Jewish leaders stress Palestinians' support of attacks," by Melissa Radler. The *Jerusalem Post,* September 13, 2001. Google users, enter: radler jewish congress jack rosen.

11. "Bush will act alone if need be, says Perle," by Toby Harnden in Washington. UK: *Telegraph,* August 9, 2002. Google users, enter: perle bush will act alone.

12. "The obscure goat story of 9-11," ecclesia.org. Google users, enter: obscure goat story bush and also card bush turned somber reading.

13. *Day of Deceit*, by Robert Stinnett. New York: Simon and Schuster, 2001. Google users, enter: robert stinnett pearl harbor.

14. "How George Bush Earned His Summer Vacation," by James Carney and John Dickerson. *Time* magazine, August 5, 2001. Google users, enter: longest vacation in presidential history.

15. "Targeting Iraq: US hypocrisy and media lies," by Sharon Smith. *International Socialist Review*, November–December 2001.

16. JINSA Report # 321, March 28, 2003 - www.jinsa.org.

17. "US draws up secret plan to impose regime on Iraq," Brian Whitaker and Luke Harding in Sulaimaniya. *The Guardian* (UK), Tuesday April 1, 2003.

18. *Commentary* magazine, Norman Podhoretz. Google: podhoretz world war iv.

20. Interview with Mike Ruppert, from The Wilderness.

21. Tariq Azis interview with Dan Rather, CBS News, August 20, 2002. Google users, enter: tariq aziz dan rather.

22. "How Israel Is Wrapped Up in Iraq," by Joe Klein. *Time*. Wednesday, Feb. 05, 2003.

23. *White Man's Burden*, by Ari Shavit. *Ha'artez*. April 5, 2003. http://www.haaretz.com/hasen/pages/ShArt.jhtml? itemNo= 280279&contrassID=2&subContrassID=14&sbSubContrass ID=0&listSrc=Y

24. Ibid.

25. "In the pipeline: More regime change," by Hooman Peimani. *Asia Times*, quoting *Ha'aretz*, April 4, 2003.

26. "For Israel Lobby Group, War Is Topic A, Quietly," by Dana Milbank, *Washington Post* Staff Writer, *Washington Post*, Tuesday, April 1, 2003, page A25.

27. Ibid.

CHAPTER 23

1. Ben Franklin, Historical Review of Pennsylvania, 1759. Google: Benjamin Franklin essential liberty.

2. "Privacy's Out When You Are A Suspect," by William Safire. *New York Times*, 11-15-02.

3. See the logo at TIA's own website ... http://www.darpa.mil/iao/.

4. Statement of Senator Patrick Leahy, The Homeland Security Department Act, November 19, 2002. www.senate.gov.
5. "The Truth about Arlen Specter," by Mary Tracy. Google http://www.geocities.com/justicewell/specter.htm by: magic bullet arlen specter.
6. See Chapter 17, Footnote #4.

CHAPTER 24

1. "The Father of Spin: Edward L. Bernays & the Birth of PR," *Quarter*, 1999. Google users, enter: Edward Bernays father of spin.

WASHINGTON'S FAREWELL ADDRESS

1. "Washington's Farewell Address." Google users, enter: washington's farewell address.

If You Liked This Book, You Won't Want To Miss Other Titles By Dandelion Books

Non-Fiction:

Palestine & The Middle East: Passion, Power & Politics, by Jaffer Ali ... The Palestinian struggle is actually a human one that transcends Palestine ... There is no longer a place for Zionism in the 20th century ... Democracy in the Middle East is mot safe for US interests as long as there is an atmosphere of hostility ... Suicide bombings are acts of desperation and mean that a people have been pushed to the brink ... failure to understand why they happen will make certain they will continue. Jaffer Ali is a Palestinian-American business man who has been writing on politics and business for over 25 years. (ISBN 1893302474)

America, Awake! We Must Take Back Our Country, by Norman D. Livergood ... This book is intended as a wake-up call for Americans, as Paul Revere awakened the Lexington patriots to the British attack on April 18, 1775, and as Thomas Paine's *Common Sense* roused apathetic American colonists to recognize and struggle against British oppression. Our current situation is similar to that which American patriots faced in the 1770s: a country ruled by 'foreign' and 'domestic' plutocratic powers and a divided citizenry uncertain of their vital interests. (ISBN 189330227X)

The Awakening of An American: How America Broke My Heart, by Meria Heller, with a Foreword by Catherine Austin Fitts ... A collection of choice interviews from Meria Heller's world-famous www.meria.net rapidly growing radio network that reaches millions of people daily. Dr. Arun Gandhi, Greg Palast, Vincent Bugliosi, Mark Elsis, William Rivers Pitt, Mark Rechtenwald, Nancy Oden & Bob Fertik, Howard Winant, Linda Starr, Dave Chandler, Bev Conover, John Nichols, Robert McChesney, Norman Solomon, Stan Goff and Mark Crispin Miller. (ISBN 1893302393)

America's Nightmare: The Presidency of George Bush II, by John Stanton & Wayne Madsen ... Media & Language, War & Weapons, Internal Affairs and a variety of other issues pointing out the US "crisis without precedent" that was wrought by the US Presidential election of 2000 followed by 9/11. "Stanton & Madsen will challenge many of the things you've been told by CNN and Fox news. This book is dangerous." (ISBN 1893302296)

America's Autopsy Report, by John Kaminski ... The false fabric of history is unraveling beneath an avalanche of pathological lies to justify endless war and Orwellian new laws that revoke the rights of Americans. While TV and newspapers glorify the dangerous ideas of perverted billionaires, the Internet has pulsated with outrage and provided a new and real forum for freedom among concerned people all over the world who are opposed to the mass murder and criminal exploitation of the defenseless victims of multinational corporate totalitarianism. John Kaminski's passionate essays give voice to those hopes and fears of humane people that are ignored by the big business shysters who rule the major media. (ISBN 1893302423)

Seeds Of Fire: China And The Story Behind The Attack On America, by Gordon Thomas ... The inside story about China that no one can afford to ignore. Using his unsurpassed contacts in Israel, Washington, London and Europe, Gordon Thomas, internationally acclaimed best-selling author and investigative reporter for over a quarter-century, reveals information about China's intentions to use the current crisis to launch itself as a super-power and become America's new major enemy ... "This has been kept out of the news agenda because it does not suit certain business interests to have that truth emerge ... Every patriotic American should buy and read this book ... it is simply revelatory." (Ray Flynn, Former U.S. Ambassador to the Vatican) (ISBN 1893302547)

Shaking The Foundations: Coming Of Age In The Postmodern Era, by John H. Brand, D.Min., J.D. ... Scientific discoveries in the Twentieth Century require the restructuring of our understanding the nature of Nature and of human beings. In simple language the author explains how significant implications of quantum mechanics, astronomy, biology and brain physiology form the foundation for new perspectives to comprehend the meaning of our lives. (ISBN 1893302253)

Rebuilding The Foundations: Forging A New And Just America, by John H. Brand, D.Min., J.D. ... "Should we expect a learned scholar to warn us about our dangerous reptilian brains that are the real cause of today's evils? Although Brand is not without hope for rescuing America, he warns us to act fast-and now. Evil men intent on imposing their political, economic, and religious self-serving goals on America are not far from achieving their goal of mastery." (ISBN 1893302334)

Democracy Under Siege: The Jesuits' Attempt To Destroy the Popular Government Of The United States; The True Story Of Abraham Lincoln's Death; Banned For Over 100 Years, This Information Now Revealed For The First Time! by C.T. Wilcox ... U.S. President Lincoln was the triumphant embodiment of the New Concept of Popular Government. Was John Wilkes Booth a Jesuit patsy, hired to do the dirty work for the Roman Catholic church – whose plan, a well-kept secret until now – was to overthrow the American Government? (ISBN 1893302318)

The Last Atlantis Book You'll Ever Have To Read! by Gene D. Matlock ... More than 25,000 books, plus countless other articles have been written about a fabled confederation of city-states known as Atlantis. If it really did exist, where was it located? Does anyone have valid evidence of its existence – artifacts and other remnants? According to historian, archaeologist, educator and linguist Gene D. Matlock, both questions can easily be answered. (ISBN 1893302202)

The Last Days Of Israel, by Barry Chamish ... With the Middle East crisis ongoing, *The Last Days of Israel* takes on even greater significance as an important book of our age. Barry Chamish, investigative reporter who has the true story about Yitzak Rabin's assassination, tells it like it is. (ISBN 1893302164)

The Courage To Be Who I Am, by Mary-Margareht Rose ... This book is rich with teachings and anecdotes delivered with humor and humanness, by a woman who followed her heart and learned to listen to her inner voice; in the process, transforming every obstacle into an opportunity to test her courage to manifest her true identity. (ISBN 189330213X)

The Making Of A Master: Tracking Your Self-Worth, by Jeanette O'Donnal ... A simple tracking method for self-improvement that takes the mystery out of defining your goals, making a road map and tracking your progress. A book rich with nuggets of wisdom couched in anecdotes and instructive dialogues. (ISBN 1893302369)

The Clear and Simple Way is a book about heart, with heart. Using the metaphor and imagery of angels, author Judith A. Parsons, known throughout the world for her spiritual workshops and seminars, shows us how to transform our lives into infinite "presents"—"gifts" and moment-by-moment experiences—of peace, joy and self-fulfillment. (ISBN 1893302431)

Fiction:

The Alley of Wishes, by Laurel Johnson ... Despite the ravages of World War I on Paris and on the young American farm boy, Beck Sanow, and despite the abusive relationship that the chanteuse Cerise endures, the two share a bond that is unbreakable by time, war, loss of memory, loss of life and loss of youth. Beck and Cerise are both good people beset by constant tragedy. Yet it is tragedy that brings them together, and it is unconditional love that keeps them together. (ISBN 1893302466)

Freedom: Letting Go Of Anxiety And Fear Of The Unknown, by Jim Britt ... Jeremy Carter, a fireman from Missouri who is in New York City for the day, decides to take a tour of the Trade Center, only to watch in shock, the attack on its twin towers from a block away. Afterward as he gazes at the pit of rubble and talks with many of the survivors, Jeremy starts to explore the inner depths of his soul, to ask questions he'd never asked before. This dialogue helps him learn who he is and what it takes to overcome the fear, anger, grief and anxiety this kind of tragedy brings. (ISBN 1893302741)

The Prince Must Die, by Gower Leconfield ... breaks all taboos for mystery thrillers. After the "powers that be" suppressed the manuscripts of three major British writers, Dandelion Books breaks through with a thriller involving a plot to assassinate Prince Charles. *The Prince Must Die* brings to life a Britain of today that is on the edge with race riots, neo-Nazis, hard right backlash and neo-punk nihilists. Riveting entertainment ... you won't be able to put it down. (ISBN 1893302725)

Waaaay Out There, by Tuklo Nashoba ... Adventures of constable Clint Mankiller and his deputy, Chad GhostWolf; Jim Bob and Bubba Johnson, Grandfather GhostWolf, Cassie Snodgrass, Doc Jones, Judge Jenkins and the rest of the Diggertown, Oklahoma bunch in the first of a series of Big Foot-Sasquatch tall tales peppered with lots of good belly laughs and just as much fun. (ISBN 189330244X)

Daniela, by Stephen Weeks ... A gripping epic novel of sexual obsession and betrayal as Nazi Prague falls. The harboring of deadly secrets and triumph of an enduring love against the hardest of times. Nikolei is a Polish/Ukrainian Jew who finds himself fighting among the Germans then turning against them to save Prague in 1945. Nikolei manages to hide himself among the Germans with a woman working as a prostitute. (ISBN 1893302377)

Unfinished Business, by Elizabeth Lucas Taylor ... Lindsay Mayer knows something is amiss when her husband, Griffin, a college professor, starts spending too much time at his office and out-of-town. Shortly after the ugly truth surfaces, Griffin disappears altogether. Lindsay is shattered. Life without Griffin is life without life ... One of the sexiest books you'll ever read! (ISBN 1893302687)

The Woman With Qualities, by Sarah Daniels ... South Florida isn't exactly the Promised Land that forty-nine-year-old newly widowed Keri Anders had in mind when she transplanted herself here from the northeast ... A tough action-packed novel that is far more than a love story. (ISBN 1893302113)

Weapon In Heaven, by David Bulley ... Eddy Licklighter is in a fight with God for his very own soul. You can't mess around half-assed when fighting with God.

You've got to go at it whole-hearted. Eddy loses his wife and baby girl in a fire. Bulley's protagonist is a contemporary version of the Old Testament character of Job. Licklighter wants nothing from God except His presence so he can kill him off. The humor, warmth, pathos and ultimate redemption of Licklighter will make you hold your sides with laughter at the same time you shed common tears for his "God-awful" dilemma. (ISBN 1893302288)

Adventure Capital, by John Rushing ... South Florida adventure, crime and violence in a fiction story based on a true life experience. A book you will not want to put down until you reach the last page. (ISBN 1893302083)

A Mother's Journey: To Release Sorrow And Reap Joy, by Sharon Kay ... A poignant account of Norah Ann Mason's life journey as a wife, mother and single parent. This book will have a powerful impact on anyone, female or male, who has experienced parental abuse, family separations, financial struggles and a desperate need to find the magic in life that others talk about that just doesn't seem to be there for them. (ISBN 1893302520)

Diving Through Clouds, by Nicola Lindsay ... Kate is dying ... dying ... dead; but not quite. Total demise would have deprived her guardian angel, Thomas, from taking her on a nose-dive through the clouds of self-denial to see herself in the eyes of the friends and family she left behind. A spiritual journey from a gifted fiction writer. (ISBN 1893302199)

Return To Masada, by Robert G. Makin ... In a gripping account of the famous Battle of Masada, Robert G. Makin skillfully recaptures the blood and gore as well as the spiritual essence of this historic struggle for freedom and independence. (ISBN 1893302105)

Time Out Of Mind, by Solara Vayanian ... Atlantis had become a snake pit of intrigue teeming with factious groups vying for power and control. An unforgettable drama that tells of the breakdown of the priesthood, the hidden scientific experiments in genetic engineering which produced "things" – part human and part animal – and other atrocities; the infiltration by the dark lords of Orion; and the implantation of the human body with a device to fuel the Orion wars. (ISBN 1893302210)

ALL DANDELION BOOKS ARE AVAILABLE THROUGH WWW.DANDELIONBOOKS.NET ... ALWAYS.

CPSIA information can be obtained at www.ICGtesting.com
Printed in the USA
LVOW08s0743270813

349698LV00001B/47/A